School-Based Clinics, The Abortion Connection

School-Based Clinics, The Abortion Connection

Richard D. Glasow, Ph. D.

Foreword by
Jo Ann Gasper
Former Deputy Assistant Secretary for Population Affairs
U.S. Department of Health and Human Services

National Right to Life Educational Trust Fund
Washington, D.C. 1988

National Right to Life
Educational Trust Fund
419 Seventh Street, N.W., Suite 500
Washington, D.C. 20004

90   5 4 3 2

Library of Congress Cataloging-in-Publication Data

Glasow, Richard D., 1945-
  School-based clinics, The Abortion Connection.

  Bibliography: p.

  1. Birth control clinics—United States.
  2. Pregnant schoolgirls—Services for—United States.
  3. Abortion—United States.   3. Pro-life movement—United States.   I. Title.
LB3432.5.G58   1988   371.7'12   87-35033
ISBN 0-9619452-0-6

Credits:

  Cover and book design by: Bergel art/media
  Cover photo illustration by: Rolando Garcés
  Composition by: Reston Graphics, Inc.

DEDICATION

Dedicated to my parents

Richard K. Glasow (1919-1969) and Dolores Glasow Warner

TABLE OF CONTENTS

FOREWORD

School-Based Clinics; The Abortion Connection is a much needed book and should be read by everyone who wants to know the truth about school-based clinics. This book exposes the motives behind school-based clinics, and it explains the way schools are being used to encourage children to kill their unborn children.

"Children having children" is decried by many. It is indeed unfortunate that so many children are engaging in premarital sexual activity and becoming pregnant. However, the solution for "children having children" should not be helping one child to arrange for the death of another child.

And yet, there has recently been a rapid expansion of school-based clinics which increase abortion and do not reduce adolescent pregancy. One major reason for this rapid expansion is that many parents and educators have been led to believe that school-based clinics will reduce adolescent pregnancy and improve the health of school children. These may both be laudatory goals in and of themselves. However, before subjecting school children to unproven and experimental programs, prudent parents and educators need to consider both the message that school-based clinics send to students as well as the facts regarding whether or not these clinics actually reduce adolescent pregnancy.

Peter Drucker, a leading management expert, has indicated that the most important question in organization or company can ask itself is "What business am I in?" When that question is answered, he advised that the organization should never loose track of the business it is in and should make sure that its efforts and activities further that endeavour. Schools are in the business of education. Their job is to support parents in the education of children, and to inculcate in students the love of knowledge and truth. Thus, on philosophical grounds, school-based clinics are pernicious. They detract from and dilute what schools should be doing. A school is sufficiently challenged to provide a substantive education in math, English, history, science as well as assisting with the development of the student's character. Schools must competently discharge their primary responsibility without being diverted by other activities.

Unfortunately, too many schools have lost their focus on their primary mission—education. School-based clinics further fragment the resources of the school. Schools should specialize in what they have been charged by parents to do. Additional fragmentation is a disservice both to parents and to students. Schools cannot effectively do their most important mission of achieving excellence in education and at the same time be a "one-stop center" for all of the social problems a community may have. Schools need to be centers for learning.

School-based clinics also send a wrong message to children. Although the so-called "comprehensive" clinics are sold to parents and schools on the basis of their providing a broad range of health services, the only service which is almost universally provided is "reproductive health" services or "family planning." Most family planning providers are strongly committed to promoting and encouraging abortion without parental knowledge or consent. The establishment of clinics which counsel, refer and assist children to obtain abortions is an admission on the part of parents and educators that if a teenager has an unplanned pregnancy, her taking of the life of her unborn child is an appropriate "solution". The moral authority of schools should not be used to indicate that abortion is in the best interest of a child.

School-based clinics are tantamount to moral surrender—something which adults simply cannot do. Children deserve the best. Parents and educators should be committed to assisting children to learn. Schools must ensure that children have learned how to read, write, and compute. These skills are necessary for a student to be able to achieve her potential. Furthermore, schools cannot and should not abandon children. Adults simply cannot say to a child—"I give up. I can't teach you right from wrong."

Although school-based clinics are the wrong remedy on philosophical grounds, Dr. Richard Glasow in *School-Based Clinics, The Abortion Connection* has insightfully shown the pragmatic problems with school-based clinics. Lest anyone mistake what I am saying—schools have for a long time provided fundamental health services. School nurses and aides have worked with parents to ensure that sick children are sent home, that medications prescribed by the family physician are provided during the school day, and minor scrapes and bruises are properly treated.

So-called "comprehensive" school-based clinics are different. Any parent or school administrator who is considering permitting a school-based clinics within their school should ask some tough questions regarding the clinics: For example, ask, who is pushing comprehensive clinics and why? Do the clinics reduce adolescent sexual activity and subsequent pregnancy or do the facilities reduce the number of babies born to school children because more abortions are performed on students?

School-Based Clinics, The Abortion Connection points out not only the conflict of interest which advocates for school-based clinics have, but shows that school-based clinics do not reduce adolescent pregnancy It has been repeatedly documented that school-based clinics do reduce the *birth rate.* The birth rate reduction occurs because the *abortion rate increases.*

Advocates for school-based clinics have indicated that they want a school-based clinic to improve the health of children. Although this may be a laudatory goal in itself, one must question why advocates frequently remove their support when the school-based clinic is not permitted to provide "reproductive health" services—bureaucratic language for abortion counseling and referral.

Dr. Glasow shows how school-based clinics, even though they do not reduce teenage pregnancies, they do reduce parental authority. School-based clinics drive a wedge between the parent and the child. Advocates for school-based clinics say that they get parental permission, yet Dr. Glasow has pointed out how that is rarely the case. Furthermore, if certain federal program dollars are used, requiring parental knowledge or consent may be prohibited.

Although school-based clinics are usually started with a significant amount of private foundation money and sometimes a small amount of state and federal dollars, inevitably the total cost of the clinics will be borne by the taxpayer. The private foundations are interested in getting the clinics started, but private foundation dollars will not continue to support the clinics over the long term. Once the clinic has opened in a school, it will be almost impossible to remove it because it will have acquired a constituency. When the private dollars stop supporting the clinic, the taxpayers will have to pick up the cost. The cost to the taxpayer may be enormous not only because of the expensive nature of the program but also because of the potential for liability.

School-based clinics do not solve the problem of adolescent pregnancy, but increase abortions and undercut parental rights. These facilities send the wrong message to students and should not be where they can have such an adverse influence on teenagers. National Right to Life has done a tremendous service for educators, parents, and students by exposing the truth about school-based clinics.

Jo Ann Gasper
Former Deputy Assistant Secretary
for Population Affairs, U.S. Department
of Health and Human Services

This foreword was written by Jo Ann Gasper in her private capacity. No official support or endorsement by any federal agency is intended or should be inferred.

ACKNOWLEDGEMENTS

I am indebted to the leaders of National Right to Life, John C. Willke, M.D., president, David N. O'Steen, Ph.D., executive director, and Darla St. Martin, associate executive director, for both their unswerving support for the research and writing of this book and their excellent editorial comments on the manuscript as it went through various stages.

I am particularly indebted to Dave Andrusko, editor of the *National Right to Life News,* who provided indispensible encouragement and insightful editorial comments on draft after draft of this book. Gary Bergel deserves a vote of thanks for his outstanding work on the design and layout of the cover and text. I also thank my assistant, Clare Richter, and my secretary, Marie Hagan, for shouldering the responsibilities of the National Right to Life Education Department while I was writing.

My largest debt of gratitude goes to my wife, Suzanne, and our children, David and Kathleen, for their steady support and patient understanding.

Lastly, I wish to express my appreciation to the local and state pro-life leaders whose inquiries to National Right to Life about this latest pro-abortion threat stimulated the research which culminated in this publication. I sincerely hope that this book will assist them in their vitally important grassroots educational work.

INTRODUCTION

N o issue that cuts as close to the nerve as abortion could be in the public domain for more than twenty years without proponents and opponents constantly coming up with new tactics to either expand or restrict abortion. Without question the most creative and invidious ploy ever by abortion partisans to multiply the numbers of abortions secured by teenagers is the rise of the so-called School-based Clinics (SBCs). Packaged as a good faith effort to provide "comprehensive" health-care services to medically under-served inner-city youths, in reality SBCs represent a wish come true for abortion proponents and others who for decades have dreamt of direct access to the minds and bodies of impressionable teenagers. Even a cursory glance at newspaper clippings assembled from around the country illustrate the success of SBC proponents. The number of operational clinics increased by over 400% in less than three years, from 23 in the fall of 1984 to 101 in the fall of 1987. Moreover, there are plans for at least another 100 on the drawing boards. Support for SBCs has come from the highest councils, including the prestigious and influential National Academy of Sciences. (Lovick and Wesson 1986, 1; Lovick 1987c, 4; Seligmann 1987, 54).*

It was not just the impeccable pro-abortion credentials of the major forces behind SBCs—the Planned Parenthood Federation of America, the Center for Population Options, and the like—that initially aroused pro-life suspicions. As we attended the meetings and read their publications, it became clear that SBC advocates were involved in a conscious sophisticated plan to deliberately mislead the public. The promotion of abortion—denied feverishly in public— was affirmed over and over privately when they gathered together to discuss strategy.

SBC champions are exploiting our collective anxiety over the high number of teen pregnancies, almost half of which end in abortion, to advance their own particular agenda. Once we understand who is behind SBCs, how SBCs have and will be used to promote and refer for abortion, and what misleading claims proponents have made about the alleged success of SBCs in reducing

---

*A list of the references used begins on page 127.

the incidence of adolescent pregnancies, we will be in a position to cut through the fog of statistics and claims cultivated by SBC proponents as they try to plant clinics in our schools.

Reasons for Growth

How can we best explain the rapid growth and avalanche of support for SBCs? Three reasons, primarily, seem to be the cause.

Concern About Teen Pregnancies and Abortion

First, the Planned Parenthood Federation and its allies have capitalized on genuine public concern over the high numbers of adolescent pregnancies, a very large percentage of which end in abortions. A couple of words to illustrate the magnitude of the problem are in order. (A more comprehensive analysis which includes detailed statistical tables is available in Appendix One.)

During 1983, the latest year for which reliable statistics are available, 1,072,293 adolescent girls became pregnant. Forty-seven percent gave birth; forty percent obtained abortions; and an estimated thirteen percent miscarried.

Among the 499,038 girls who gave birth (or 46.7 percent of the total pregnant), about half were married and half unmarried. A pregnant teenager who is married is much more likely to give birth than to have an abortion, while just the opposite is true for unmarried teenagers.

Unfortunately, 427,680 (or 40 percent) of the total number of pregnant teens aborted their children—1,172 teen abortions every day. Ninety-six percent of these teen abortions were performed on unmarried girls, who in 1983 experienced more abortions than births.

Teenagers abort a higher proportion of their pregnancies than any other age group, except women age forty and older. To put this number into some perspective, it is important to keep in mind that women in that older age group have less than 2% of the annual total number of abortions (Henshaw 1987, 7).

Long-range trends hold out little promise for significant improvement. Since the early 1970s, the number of births to teenagers has steadily gone down, primarily due to an increase in abortions. In fact, the number of teen abortions almost doubled during the decade following the 1973 *Roe v. Wade* decision (Hoffreth and Hayes 1987, A62/414-A63/415). The annual total of abortions on girls ages 15 through 19 increased from 232,440 abortions in 1973 to 418,740 in 1982.

With abortions becoming more common, not surprisingly, the rate of repeat abortions continues to mount (Hofferth and Hayes 1987, A79/431). Finally, teens procure a disproportionate number of post-twelve-week abortions, which are both more dangerous to the girl's life and health and endanger her prospects for future childbearing.

"Recent research has shown that there are many long-term devastating emotional and psychological effects of abortion," explained Kay James, president of Black Americans for Life, in an article in the Congressional Black Caucus magazine (James 1987, 26). This phenomena, identified as Post Abortion Syndrome, James stated, "may include guilt, anxiety, depression, increase in drug and alcohol abuse, as well as suicidal tendencies."

Growing Desperation

The second reason why momentum for school-based clinics has built up quickly is that policy-makers are so desperate for a "solution" to teen pregnancies and abortion that they uncritically accept the claims of the SBC advocates. So intense is public concern over teen pregnancy that otherwise cautious people will ignore the tough political, social, and moral questions that would normally be asked before such expensive and invasive government programs were established. But, in a sense, this unwillingness to pause is also due to the lack, until recently, both of academic evidence to contradict the claims of SBC supporters and of organized grassroots opposition to their campaign.

Misleading Tactics

The third and most important reason SBC proponents have been so successful is a strategy of deception and misrepresentation. Clearing away the smokescreens is the principal focus of this book. Citing the SBC proponents' own publications and speeches, each chapter of this book examines a different facet of the clinic promoters' attempts to mislead the public and policymakers about their actual agenda and the pro-abortion implications of SBCs.

Chapter One describes the radical alterations that SBC supporters propose to make in the way that schools currently offer "health" services. Major changes in the staffing, types of services, and sponsorship provide the institutional structure for promoting abortion. The Planned Parenthood Federation and its allies get the public's attention with claims that SBCs can ameliorate the teen pregnancy problem, but when opposition develops to that agenda, they utilize the so-called "comprehensive" services as a ruse to get their pro-abortion programs into schools. Joy Dryfoos, one of the nation's leading experts and advocates of SBCs, explained at a conference in June 1987 that "as long as you don't ask the schools to provide the services but simply get the school's approval to let other groups in who will provide the [medical and educational] services, then you can do all kinds of things in schools that you never dreamed of" (Quoted in Coughlan 1987b).

Chapter Two goes to the heart of the pro-life opposition to SBCs. It contrasts the professed claims by clinic advocates that their facilities do not promote abortion with actual SBC policies which facilitate—indeed promote—abortion counseling, abortion referrals, and pro-abortion "sex education." In the understated words of Joy Dryfoos, "the issue of abortion is frequently finessed in the clinics" (Dryfoos 1985b, 75).

That they would use such underhanded methods to put abortion into the schools should not come as a surprise in view of the long history of pro-abortion advocacy by leading SBC proponents. Chapter Three explodes their "myth of neutrality" by exposing how they package propaganda and selective interpretation as objective research.

Chapter Four reveals the stark contrast between the SBC advocates' public justifications for establishing clinics and what they discuss privately among themselves. They expect that school clinics will enable them to achieve long-standing ideological and financial goals.

Chapter Five closely scrutinizes how SBC proponents have greatly misrepresented their alleged "successes" in reducing teen abortions by reducing teen pregnancies. Their statistical data cannot support their overblown claims, and, if anything, the evidence from two clinics in Michigan and Missouri leads to the conclusion that SBCs increase, rather than decrease, abortions. Moreover, this chapter describes how supporters of SBCs have tried to shift the measurement of success from reducing the number of teen pregnancies to less meaningful, when not meaningless, measurements, such as attendance at the clinic.

Pro-life supporters are particularly sensitive to the issues of parental rights since abortionists routinely perform abortions on minor girls without parental knowledge or consent. Therefore, in Chapter Six, we look at how SBCs undermine parental authority and responsibility by administering pregnancy tests, performing counselling, and referring minor daughters for abortions—all typically without parental knowledge or consent.

In Chapter Seven, we describe five major issues that bring into serious question the case for opening clinics, issues which SBC proponents attempt to softpedal as "tangential" to the "core" issues they want to discuss. Critics have raised questions about the high expense and low cost-effectiveness of SBCs, the inevitable demand for government funding once the limited private funding runs out, and the need for extensive medical liability insurance coverage by clinics.

Moreover, both parents and leading policymakers, such as U.S. Secretary of Education William Bennett, are worried that the SBCs may cause a further deterioration in the quality of education in the already overburdened school system. Finally, opponents of SBCs, both White and Black, have pointed out the clear-cut evidence of the racism implicit in a strategy which targets Blacks and other minorities by placing SBCs almost exclusively in inner-city schools.

As described in Chapter Eight, the growing public awareness of these serious drawbacks during 1985 and 1986 caused a groundswell of community opposition. By working with coalitions of individuals and organizations, well-informed and strongly motivated pro-life advocates have spearheaded effective efforts to stop or delay establishment of clinics in many cities across the county, including Cincinnati, San Diego, Miami, and Boston. Their most effective tactic to deflate the SBC advocates' exaggerated claims was to use their own words against them.

Chapter Nine suggests that the future for SBCs might not be as bright as proponents believe because of the growing, but largely unpublicized, grass-roots resistance. As anti-SBC educational and organizational work becomes more effective and widespread, local opposition will very likely further slow the pro-clinic movement's momentum by either preventing clinics from opening or severely restricting their activities, especially in regard to abortion.

CHAPTER ONE

WHAT IS A "SCHOOL-BASED CLINIC?"

S chool nurses have offered a laudatory health service to public and private secondary school students for decades, and during the last ten years, some states have initiated improvements in school health facilities. However, none of the proposals was as radical as the changes urged by SBC advocates.

Their proposed alterations in sponsorship, staffing, and services provide the organizational structure for in-school clinics to promote abortion. Although they claim the so-called "comprehensive" package of services is vital to the medically underserved inner-city teenagers, critics point out the principal aim of the SBC is to lure students into the clinic for reproductive health services.

The medical and educational services may be offered in facilities either inside the school in a "school-based clinic" or adjacent to the school, in what would more appropriately be called a "school-linked clinic." For our purposes here, both types will be referred to as "SBCs."

Sponsorship By Outside Agencies

The first distinctive feature of SBCs is sponsorship. According to Asta Kenney, a researcher with the Alan Guttmacher Institute, the Planned Parenthood Federation's research arm, they "are usually organized by an outside organization or group (such as a health department, hospital or private non-profit organization) that lays the groundwork for the clinic in the community and provides the expertise, staff and insurance" (Kenney 1986a, 44). "The school typically contributes the space and facilitates attendance," she said. For example, in the widely emulated St. Paul, Minnesota program, the St. Paul-Ramsey Medical Center operated the clinic from 1973 until mid-1986, when a separate non-profit corporation took over (Ahartz 1986, 13-14). In other cities, different types of medical agencies are sponsors: a community health clinic (Jackson-Hinds in Jackson, Mississippi), a private non-profit corporation under contract with the city health department (DuSable in south Chicago), a private non-profit organization (Kansas City, Missouri and Houston, Texas), and a family-planning clinic (Planned Parenthood in Michigan) (Kirby 1985, 9).

Staffing

A dramatic change in staffing is the second characteristic that distinguishes SBCs from traditional school medical facilities. Unlike school nurses who frequently work alone and are either school district or municipal employees, SBCs require a large staff which is paid by the outside sponsoring organization.

According to the Center for Population Options's *School-Based Health Clinics: A Guide To Implementing Programs* published in 1986, the "ideal staff" could consist of a number of part-time support workers plus the following eleven employees, who are either full- or part-time: physician, clinic administrator, nurse-practitioner, social worker, nutritionist, health educator, dentist, dental hygienist, psychologist, medical assistant, and receptionist (Hadley 1986, 62). Even in a small facility with a part-time physician and full-time nurse-practitioner, health educator, assistant, and receptionist, the salaries of these medical professionals represent the major operating cost (Ahartz 1986, 100). A functioning clinic in a medium-sized high school can easily cost $250,000 annually.

How do the current school nurses fit into these plans? Not very well, according to a series of articles by Sharon Lordi in the March/April 1987 issue of *School Nurse*, published by the National Association of School Nurses. Lordi pointed out that "school nurses have their own good reasons for feeling threatened by SBCs" (Lordi 1987b, 24). "In certain areas, SBCs have replaced preexisting school health services," she reported, "and school nurses have lost their jobs."[1]

Services

The third major change from current arrangements proposed by SBC advocates is a substantial increase in both the type and scope of services provided within schools. Practical considerations—the need to keep controversy to a minimum until the clinic is established—force SBC proponents to use "comprehensive services" as a cover story for their real agenda.

Whenever the connection between school-based clinics and abortion is raised, proponents try to avert criticism by making two contradictory assertions. On one hand, the proponents try to garner support by making excessive claims about how successful the 20 to 25 percent of the SBCs' confidential reproductive health program have been in reducing teen pregnancies (Kantrowitz 1987, 57; Wattleton 1986). (Actually, as we shall see in Chapter Five, the fragmentary statistics available about the effects of SBCs reveal that they reduce births, not pregnancies. In fact, the evidence points to a rise in abortion referrals as the cause.)

On the other hand, school-clinic supporters downplay the amount of their controversial reproductive health services and emphasize their other, non-reproductive health activities. For example, Judith Senderowitz, executive director of the Center for Population Options, stressed in an article in the *Miami Herald* on August 2, 1987 that "75 percent of the services rendered at SBCs are unrelated to reproductive health needs" (Senderowitz 1987, 4C). Sonny Gross, assistant superintendent of schools of Dade County, Florida made similar remarks that were reported in the November 11, 1986 edition of *USA Today* (Katz 1986, 2). The proposed clinics in the Miami schools would offer a variety of health services, he emphasized, including "general health exams, screening, lab services, dental hygiene and other services." Nevertheless, complained Gross, "the discussion is all about birth control and abortion."

Direct Medical Treatment

Most secondary-school nurses offer first aid and minimal preventative care, but SBCs "differ from more traditional school health programs," observed the Center for Population Option's authoritative publication "School-Based Clinics: Update 1986," "by having the authority to prescribe and/or dispense medications" (Lovick and Wesson 1986, 8). According to the booklet, SBCs provide "direct medical treatment" through a broad range of so-called "comprehensive" services commonly claims to include athletic physicals, laboratory and diagnostic screening, immunizations, prenatal and post-partum care, drug and alcohol abuse programs, and weight-reduction and nutrition programs. In most cases, such medical services require specially configured rooms, extensive supplies, and expensive equipment (Dryfoos 1985b, 72; Kirby 1985, 11).

SBCs also provide students with pregnancy testing and abortion counseling and abortion referrals, which will be analyzed in the next chapter (Dryfoos 1985b, 73).

If there can be said to have been a benefit from the controversy over SBCs, it has been to alert right-to-lifers to the necessity to check immediately if anyone in their local schools are performing abortion counseling or referrals. Inquiries by pro-lifers in New York and Pennsylvania revealed that school nurses, counselors, and teachers already have been performing abortion referrals for pregnant teenagers.

The Real Agenda

Although SBC proponents use every opportunity to proclaim that their primary objective is providing better health care for ghetto youth, they actually have dramatically different goals.

"We can talk all day about the fact that we want to open up comprehensive services," observed Sharon Lovick, one of the most knowledgeable SBC proponents, at a workshop on March 13, 1987 at the Children's Defense Fund's annual national conference on adolescent pregnancy prevention in Washington, D.C., "but the main focus—the reason people put dollars into it—still turns on the hope, the expectation, that somehow you're going to do something about adolescent pregnancy" (Lovick 1987a). As a former SBC administrator and current director of the Support Center for School-Based Clinics of the Center for Population Options, she is in a unique position to know what is happening in the SBC movement; therefore, her statements can be considered as authoritative. "The impetus for starting these [school-based] programs in most communities," Lovick candidly explained at the conference, "continues to be a goal of doing something about adolescent pregnancy" (Lovick 1987a).[2]

The next chapter examines in detail how SBCs "do something about adolescent pregnancy" by promoting abortion counseling and direct and indirect abortion referrals.

CHAPTER TWO

PROMOTING ABORTION COUNSELING AND REFERRALS, PRO-ABORTION EDUCATION, AND ABORTION PILLS

U nfortunately, many policymakers and members of the public have unthinkingly accepted claims that SBCs do not promote abortion. Illustrative of the assurances routinely given the public was the statement that appeared in the Los Angeles *Daily News* attributed to Jackie Goldberg, the Los Angeles school board member who co-authored the proposal which established two clinics. "We don't intend to have an abortion referral service in the clinic," she said. "It's really sad how a good idea can be ruined by going around and yelling abortion," she lamented (Rifkin 1986, 1).

These claims are at best half-truths. Clinic supporters recognized several years ago that their pro-abortion policies and activities posed a potentially significant public relations problem. In an important article published in March 1985 summarizing SBC activities, Joy Dryfoos observed that "the issue of abortion is frequently finessed in these clinics" (Dryfoos 1985b, 75). This choice of words and the description of SBC policies found earlier in her article would alert the reader that SBC staff members are indeed employing a "subtle and tactful strategy" (to quote the dictionary definition of "finesse"). By being less than candid, SBC proponents were able to achieve their objective of arranging for abortions without arousing the indignation of either the parents—or community.

The careful reader will find in the speeches and publications of SBC proponents explaining clinic activities clear evidence that SBCs currently encourage abortion in two ways. First, school-based clinics exploit the authority of the schools to funnel a captive clientele of pregnant teens into abortion mills without parental knowledge or consent.[1] Second, clinic staff members teach pro-abortion "sex education." In addition, the widespread establishment of SBCs could have dangerous future implications. Critics fear that if SBC advocates are successful in carrying out their plans to open clinics thoughout the country, the facilities could become distribution centers for the abortion pill, RU 486, if it eventually reaches the market in the United States.

Direct Involvement in Abortions

The principal pro-life objection to school-based clinics is that they "counsel" and "refer" pregnant girls for abortions. In this section, we will explain what those terms mean. We will also offer evidence from speeches and publications by leading SBC advocates and staff members to demonstrate how school clinics, either openly or covertly counsel and refer for abortions.*

Defining "Counseling" and "Referral"

Defining terms is an essential first step in this controversial public-policy debate because the SBC advocates will sometimes give an erroneous impression of what services a clinic is performing by twisting the usual meaning of words, especially the terms "counsel" and "refer."

"Counseling" by SBCs means informing the pregnant girl about her "legal options"—abortion or birth—and assisting her in making a decision about what course of action to take. Counseling is usually conducted in conjunction with a laboratory test and a physical examination to confirm pregnancy (U.S. Dept. of Health and Human Services 1981; 3, 10, 12, 13).

One of the key pieces of information provided to a pregnant girl during counseling is the fact that she has the constitutionally protected right to obtain an abortion without her parents' knowledge or consent. While some states

---

*Another term figuring prominently in this discussion is "performing" (or "providing") abortion which means the intentional killing of the unborn child either by dismembering the baby by sharp instruments or by injecting toxic chemicals. At this writing, no school-based clinic performs abortions (Hadley 1986, 34). However, some organizations which sponsor school-based clinics do. For example, the St. Paul-Ramsey Hospital Center in St. Paul, Minnesota, which operated several of the most widely emulated SBCs from 1973 through 1986, performs both first- and second-trimester abortions.

require nominal parental notification or consent, the U.S. Supreme Court has ruled that the girl can bypass her parents by going before a judge (Morrissey 1986, 68-69).

SBC staff members either counsel pregnant girls in their own clinic, or if prohibited from so doing, "refer" the teens to an outside organization who will "counsel" the girl, including telling her that about the "option" of abortion.

"Referral," thus, describes the process of sending the girl to an agency outside of the school to obtain services that the SBC does not provide. (U.S. Dept. of Health and Human Services 1981, 7-8, 13). The staff refers the girls out when the SBC either does not want to provide a certain service itself (such as performing abortions) or is prohibited from providing a service (such as being involved with abortion-related activities).

In addition to "referring" for "counseling," SBCs also refer for abortions— either directly or indirectly. When the rules permit, SBCs will refer pregnant teenaged girls directly to an abortion provider in the community. (Right-to-life advocates usually connect the word "referral" solely with this type of activity since the national family-planning industry operates in this way.) This referral might consist of giving the girl the name and location of the abortion-ist, directions to the office, the hours of operation, and information about possible sources of funding for the abortion, such as Medicaid or loans.

An example of this appeared in a story in the *New York Times* on October 15, 1986. It explained how Fran Combe, the resident nurse practitioner in the clinic located in Martin Luther King Jr. High School in Manhattan, made seven abortion referrals during one school year (Perlez 1986c). According to the *Times*, five of the ten girls who were found to be pregnant at Combe's clinic had abortions at the Eastern Women's Center, "the abortion clinic at 14 East 60th Street that she most frequently *recommends*" (emphasis added). Combe also directed two other pregnant girls to another abortion facility. (The remaining three young women had their babies.)

The second scenario obtains when the SBC staff is prevented by regulations or school policies from offering counseling and direct referrals to abortionists. In this case, they arrange what we will call an "indirect" referral for those abortion-related services. The school clinic circumvents the restrictions by sending the pregnant girl to an agency outside of the school, which is not governed by the same restrictions, such as the local Planned Parenthood, city or state public health clinic, or public hospital. There she could obtain a confidential pregnancy test, counseling about abortion, and another referral by the community-based agency to an abortionist (an abortion provider). As we shall see, SBC staff have persuaded themselves that this type of indirect referral does not violate school or parental restrictions on abortion-related activities.

SBCs Allowed to Perform Abortion
Counseling and Direct Referrals

According to SBC proponents, the laws and regulations governing a school clinic's operations determines what type of arrangements the staff makes to guarantee that pregnant girls can obtain abortions confidentially. We will initially examine two sets of reasons SBCs perform both on-site abortion counseling and direct referrals to abortionists without parental knowledge or consent. This section will also point out the flaws in the SBC proponents' flimsy justifications for their abortion counseling techniques. Then we will turn our attention to how the school-clinic staff utilizes indirect referrals to achieve the same objectives. (There are no published statistics revealing how many SBCs take either approach.)

Federal and State Requirements
Said to Mandate Abortion-Related Activities

Some SBCs justify performing controversial abortion-related activities in their own facilities on the grounds that they are obligated to do so by either state or federal law.

For example, the October 1986 issue of *Clinic News*, published by the Center for Population Options' clinic Support Center, listed thirty-three states and the District of Columbia where minors are empowered to give their own consent to obtain pregnancy tests, counseling, and referrals (Center for Pop. Options 1986a, 3).[2] In twelve of those states, the teens can consent for *all* of their own medical care.

Some key federal programs also carry similar explicit requirements. They provide a relatively small amount of the total SBC financial support nationally but have a profound influence all out of proportion to their number for two reasons.[3]

First, receipt of funds from a source such as Title X of the Public Health Service Act imposes requirements on the whole program. This provision is especially important in view of the efforts to pass new federal SBC funding that carries similar stipulations. For example, Senate Bill 1366, introduced in 1987 by Senator Edward Kennedy (D-Massachusetts) and others, would pour millions of dollars into new SBCs and would require that they perform confidential abortion counseling and referrals (U.S. Congress. Senate 1987; House 1987a and 1987b).

Likewise, according to an authoritative book by two attorneys and a pediatrician on providing confidential health care to adolescents, a SBC is legally bound to provide teenagers with confidential abortion counseling and referral if it received any funds from Titles XIX ("Title Nineteen," Medical Assistance) and XX ("Title Twenty," Aid to Families With Dependent Children) of the federal Social Security Act (Morrissey 1986, 63). The dollar amount of SBC funding from these two programs in 1986 was also rather small—about 2% of the total SBC funding (Lovick and Wesson 1986, 13). However, the income could increase in the future as more SBCs learn how to tap into these sources.

Federal programs also carry great influence for a second reason. Their operating policies determine national standards. Observed Asta Kenney, Guttmacher Institute staff member, speaking at the annual SBC conference in October 1986, the Title X program sets the standards for the entire "family planning industry," including of course SBCs. She noted that the Title X guidelines require that recipient agencies provide services to minors without parental knowledge or consent (Kenney 1986b).[4]

"Non-Directive" or "Objective" Counseling

SBC proponents assert that when the school clinics counsel pregnant girls about abortion, they employ the so-called "nondirective" methods used by Planned Parenthood and other members of the national family-planning industry funded by Title X. They claim to describe the two possible choices—abortion or birth—without promoting either one (Wattleton 1981, 23; U.S. Dept. of Health and Human Services 1981, 12, 13).

SBCs may even go so far as to state that they do not perform "abortion" counseling per se on the grounds that they present abortion merely as one "option." For example, the Center for Population Option's *School-Based Health Clinics: A Guide to Implementing Programs* avoids the word "abortion" by using the innocuous term "pregnancy counseling" which describes informing "pregnant patients" about "all of their legal options" (Hadley 1986, 89 and 34).

During policy debates, SBC advocates commonly make two misleading and inaccurate assertions about their counseling techniques. The first is that counseling can be performed in a neutral manner. The rhetoric of terms such as "non-directive" merely disguises the real agenda. "Counseling abortion would be pointless in the absence of an expectation that some women receiving such counseling will choose to have an abortion," pointed out the federal Department of Health and Human Services in its proposal on September 1, 1987 for new guidelines for counseling by Title X grantees (U.S. Dept. of Health and Human Services 1987, 33211).

Offering counseling about abortion sends the clear message to the students that both the SBC *and* the school believe that abortion is a morally acceptable and medically safe practice. In other words, abortion counseling in a SBC represents endorsement of abortion by the policymakers as a possible "choice." So-called "objective" counseling by SBCs about abortion is impossible.

The clinic personnel's second deceptive claim is that so-called "ethical" considerations compel them to counsel pregnant teenaged girls about abortion. "SBC practitioners," stated the SBC operating manual published in October 1986 by the Center for Population Options, "adhere to standards of medical ethics which state that pregnant patients are entitled to know all of their legal options [including of course, abortion]" (Hadley 1986, 34). Taking their cue from the family-planning clinics funded by Title X, the staff must provide that information and guidance, they assert, in order for the girls to give "informed consent" (Hayes 1987, 174).

Critics of this policy have pointed out two reasons why this line of argument falls apart under scrutiny. First, the proponents seriously misrepresent and subvert the traditions of the healing profession. Medical ethics place no burden on physicians and other health-care professionals to support or perform abortion—in fact, just the opposite. By embracing abortion, the SBC advocates have forsaken the traditional "sanctity of life" ethic in Western Civilization, which has encouraged doctors and nurses to protect the health and welfare of all members of the human race, both born and unborn (Wardle and Wood 1982, 141-156; U.S. Congress. Senate 1982b, 46).

Second, the events of the last fifteen years has completely destroyed the credibility of the clinic proponents' alleged interest in promoting "informed consent." Their litigation in federal and state courts has prevented enforcement of state and local laws requiring that a pregnant girl be given accurate and comprehensive information about the status of her pregnancy, the nature of the abortion procedure, and possible short- and long-term complications (Wardle and Wood 1982, 91-103; Horan, Grant, and Cunningham 1987, Appendix One).

The evidence clearly reveals that the clinic proponents' assertions about being compelled by "medical ethics" to promote abortion is a thinly veiled disguise to justify their pro-abortion ideological and political agenda.

Despite these flaws in the rationalizations justifying counseling, a review of press reports of debates about SBCs discloses that school-clinic advocates have been quite successful in using their misleading rhetoric to defuse criticism. Most of the media and public attention has focused on abortion *referrals*, possibly because *counseling* a pregnant teenager may not appear to have as direct a cause-and-effect relationship with abortion as giving her directions to the nearest abortionist.

One final point that is extremely important in connection with the requirements of state and federal law is the selective effect of the laws on SBC policies. Local elected officials and parents may not be aware that the laws would permit enforcement of parental consent regulations for some services in the school clinic (such as athletic physicals) but not for others (such as abortion counseling). In other words, the local authorities may erroneously believe that their parental consent policies control all of the clinic's activities when they actually control only part of them. The authoritative manual, *School-Based Health Clinics: A Guide for Implementing Programs*, published by the Center for Population Options, explained that "[l]aws in most states guarantee confidential family planning services to teenagers, but a different set of consent rules applies for general medical treatment" (Hadley 1986, 48). "At SBCs, staff members urge students to talk with their parents about sexual matters," states the manual, "but clinics respect the law insofar as informing parents directly about these matters" (Hadley 1986, 32).

SBC proponents may refrain from pointing out when the law conflicts with policies approved by the school board, and one wonders how many parents are informed about the potential conflicts when their school board or city council is considering opening school clinics.

Counseling and Referrals Done When Regulations Do Not Prohibit Them

A second category of clinics which provide on-site abortion counseling to pregnant teenaged girls, pointed out Asta Kenney at the SBC conference in Denver, are those which—in the absence of local or state laws or school regulations to the contrary—adopt the same policies as the Title X-funded facilities. She explained that the staff assumes that the same rules of "confidentiality" that govern family planning clinics operated *outside* the school, also apply to SBCs *within* the schools (Kenney 1986b).

This approach should not be surprising since much of the impetus for starting SBCs came from the family-planning industry, including Planned Parenthood and other Title X grantees. They are urging the SBCs to adopt the policies that they have employed for the last two decades in their facilities in the community.

According to Kenney, federal programs which provide most of the government funding, such as the federal Maternal and Child Health (MCH) block grant (Title V of the Public Health Service Act), do not have specific stipulations either requiring or prohibiting parental involvement (Kenney 1986b). According to a report compiled by the Center for Population Options during 1986, the MCH block grant provided twenty-seven percent of the funding for SBCs (Lovick and Wesson 1986, 13).

Using Indirect Referrals to Circumvent Restrictions on Counseling and Direct Referrals

When confronted with school regulations or parental prohibitions which prevent them from providing on-site pregnancy tests, abortion counseling, or direct referrals to abortionists, SBCs utilize two strategies to circumvent the restrictions to show pregnant teens how to obtain those forbidden services elsewhere.

One method is to employ the informal channels of communication within the school to inform the students where to go for pregnancy tests and abortion counseling. Speaking at a conference in San Diego in November 1986, Kathleen Arnold-Sheeran, a long-time nursing and administrative staff member of the St. Paul clinics and currently director of the National Association of School-Based Clinics, explained that the clinic staff in the St. Paul program was careful to inform students that the clinic did not offer abortion counseling because of the terms of a special federal grant from the Adolescent Family Life program under Title XX ("Title Twenty") (quoted in Patton 1986a). However, at the same time, the staff ensured that the girls knew the location of another facility nearby where they could obtain a free confidential pregnancy test and abortion referral. "We certainly talk to kids and let them know there are options available," she stated. "We just can't go into any details talking about abortions."

The result, pointed out the former SBC staffer, is that the pregnant girls who are considering abortion "don't come to us for their pregnancy tests." They went to the outside agency. This arrangement not only allowed the clinic to maintain a facade of not promoting abortion, but it also created the impression that the clinic was actually quite successful in convincing teens to give birth. Since the pregnant girls contemplating abortions avoided the SBC, almost all of the girls who received positive pregnancy tests at the clinic carried their babies to term. According to Arnold-Sheeran "[n]inety-eight percent that [sic] come in for pregnancy tests continue their pregnancy" (quoted in Patton 1986a).

In circumstances where the SBC performs abortion counseling but is prevented from referring girls directly to an abortion provider, the clinic staff uses a different plan. They direct the pregnant teens to an agency outside of the school, such as the local family planning or public health agency, which itself *does not* perform abortions. Then the outside agency, which is not covered by the school's or parents' restrictions, arranges to send the girls to another agency or facility, which *does* perform abortions.

This clever policy, while somewhat round-about, effectively accomplishes the objective. Moreover, it gives the SBC staff the semantic "out" they need because they can claim that they did not "refer" the girls to an abortion facility. Somehow the SBC staff believes that sending pregnant girls *indirectly*, rather than *directly*, to the abortionist, sufficiently changes the nature of the activity that they are off of the hook.

The director of public policy for the Center for Population Options, Jodie Levin-Epstein, explained how this duplicitous method operates in practice during her speech at the workshop at the Denver SBC meeting titled "Parents: Consent and Confidentiality" (Levin-Epstein 1986b). "In practice, it is our understanding," she said, "that where a parent has not given consent for participation in a program, or in those instances [where] there is a checkoff for a particular program and the student for whatever reason isn't supposed to be served by that [SBC] program according to the parental consent [form], *the program refers for [that] service, or handles it in whatever way has been articulated by the advisory board*" (emphasis added).

Commenting on that policy at the same workshop, Cleve Holt, a nurse practitioner with the Orr High School Clinic in Chicago, said "We do not even mention abortion in the school-based clinic. If it does come up, we refer them out. We don't talk about it" (Holt 1986). (We will mention the Orr Clinic's policy again in Chapter Eight.)

Steve Purser, health planning coordinator in charge of the Balboa High School clinic in San Francisco, gave a more extensive explanation of how this indirect abortion-referral policy operates during a workshop on March 6, 1986 at the annual meeting of the National Family Planning and Reproductive Health Association. His remarks are worth quoting at length.

Although his clinic is heavily supported by federal Title X money, which would normally require abortion referrals without parental knowledge or consent, he will not do that because "we don't want to usurp the parents' role" (Purser 1986). "The last thing you want to do," emphasized Purser, "is to have a parent sign a consent form saying I want to exclude 'x' service, then provide that service to the child." Then he went on to reveal that the actual reason for obstensibly being so respectful of the parent's wishes was pure politics. If the clinic gave unauthorized services, "[t]he school board would shut us down—literally," he stated emphatically.

Turning next to the issue of referrals, Purser asked himself the question of "What do we do if they [students] come to us and the parent says 'I don't want my child to receive family planning?' " (Purser 1986) If that situation arises (or if there is no signed consent form at all), he explained that "[t]hey are referred to a clinic that's about a mile-and-a-half from us, which is another health department clinic that provides family planning services." When the teenager is referred to the outside clinic, Purser stated, they "are no longer a student receiving health care at the high school, [instead] they become part of the [general] health systems population." Since the nearby city-operated health facility is not under the same restrictions as the school clinic, students receive medical treatment without parental knowledge or consent.

This point about the use of indirect abortion referrals should be emphasized because it is so important. *If the SBC is prohibited from sending a pregnant girl directly to an abortionist, then clinic personnel can and will circumvent the parents' wishes simply by sending her to an agency or organization outside the school which itself does not perform abortions but which will refer the girl to someone who does perform abortions.* Technically, of course, the SBC has not referred the girl *directly* for abortion.

Once a clinic opens in a school, this method for procuring abortions indirectly by utilizing referrals to outside agencies would be very difficult to identify and regulate. Moreover, if a controversy does develop over referrals, the clinic staff could raise new justifications for their actions, such as claiming that medical ethics or the students' "right to privacy" under federal, state or local laws. The best solution is to not open a school-based clinic in the first place.

Pro-Abortion "Sex Education"

In addition to referring pregnant girls for abortions both directly and indirectly, SBCs also promote abortion through their in-school education programs. The pilot programs in St. Paul and Baltimore, which have been widely emulated throughout the country, strongly emphasized the value of clinic personnel working closely with the school's health educators to develop the "reproductive health curriculum," and even to teach classes in order to establish rapport with the students (Ahartz 1986, 90; Zabin et al. 1986, 120, 125; Zabin et al. 1984, 425; Kapp 1986, 83).

This arrangement presents an extraordinary opportunity for the clinic staff to imbue the teens with pro-abortion concepts (usually described as presenting "all of the options") and to explain about the availability of pregnancy tests, of nearby abortion facilities, and of government funds to pay for abortions. Douglas Kirby, the Center for Population Option's director of research, observed that the classroom presentations "not only serve an educational function, but a *recruiting* function as well" (emphasis added; Kirby 1985, 13). SBC expert Joy Dryfoos explained that the "[c]linic staff often conduct sex education and family life [education] classes in the school, so they have ample opportunity to encourage the student in the classroom to attend the clinic" (Dryfoos 1985b, 73).

Finally, Kathleen Arnold-Sheeran, an experienced clinic nurse and administrator for thirteen years at the St. Paul clinic, stressed the importance of giving "lectures in the classes" at a workshop in San Diego in November 1986. "If you have a SBC without health education services, forget it," she emphasized. "It's no good" (quoted in Patton 1986a).

SBCs Pushing Abortion Pills

Another abortion-related issue that to date has not played a role in debates over SBCs but could be very important in the future is worth mentioning here. During 1986, the American public received its first thorough introduction to a new abortion pill, RU 486, that is being developed by a French company and tested throughout the world, including the United States. In the opinion of pill's developers, the drug has the potential to revolutionize the abortion debate by making early abortion an entirely private matter. The promoters have attempted to give the false impression that the pill is a contraceptive, but it is clearly an abortifacient (Kaye 1986, 14; Baulieu 1985, 1-25; Franklin 1986, 24).

The manufacturer expects to market RU 486 in France soon as a method to induce abortion within two weeks after the woman has missed her first menstrual period—in other words, when she is about four-to-six-weeks pregnant. Supporters of the pill in the U.S., such as the Population Council, project that it could be marketed here within five years, but they are encountering difficulty convincing a domestic drug company to assume the costs, especially the anticipated high expenses for liability (Knox 1986, 10; Brody 1986, A27).

The potential for distributing the abortion pill to teenagers through school clinics was not lost on SBC proponents. In a story appearing in the *Boston Globe* on December 22, 1986, the chairman of Planned Parenthood Federation's Board of Directors, Dr. Allan Rosenfield, endorsed approval of RU 486 as a "major step forward for teenagers" (Franklin 1986, 1 and 14). He believed, reported the *Globe*, that if teenaged girls who suspected they were pregnant "knew they could come to a clinic for a pill when their period is late, they would probably show up a lot earlier than they do now." Jonathan Brant, Boston attorney specializing in health care issue, explained to the *Globe* that "[m]ost current restrictions, such as parental notification laws, would be unenforceable."

The French abortion pill, RU 486, is not presently ready for introduction in the U.S., but it represents only the tip of the iceberg. Research is underway on many other chemical abortion methods. In almost every case, there is very limited information about the short-term side effects, and absolutely no data on the long-term ramifications of any of these new drugs (Spitz and Bardin 1985, 260-262; Baulieu 1985, 1 and 19).

Clearly clinics located inside of schools would be in an especially advantageous position to distribute abortion pills; therefore, one wonders whether clinics, in whatever current benign form that they make take at the moment, should be allowed to become entrenched so close to teenagers.

Abortion Connection Overlooked

Pro-life advocates should realize that debates over whether to distribute contraceptives in school clinics have in large measure overshadowed concerns over the much less public activity of abortion counseling and referrals and pro-abortion classroom instruction which routinely go on in SBCs.

The controversy in New York City is a case in point. On October 5, 1986, members of the Board of Education were embarrassed to learn through front-page newspaper stories that nine school clinics had been operating for up to two years without their knowledge and approval (Perlez 1986a to 1986g). In response to the public outcry, which focused primarily on the distribution of contraceptives without parental knowledge, the Board worked out a "compromise" modification of the policies in order to placate outraged parents. However, no one raised a question about the clinics remaining open within the schools to continue operating as abortion-referral agencies.

After a series of confrontations in cities around the country where the contraceptive debate became a lightning rod for community and parental opposition, clinic advocates have looked for ways to head off the conflict yet still stay in the schools where they can counsel and refer for abortions. "Be willing to make compromises," stressed Kathleen Arnold-Sheeran, current director of the National Association of School-Based Clinics, but "do not compromise on being in the school." Once the clinic opens, she explained, other services can be added afterward as they were in the Kansas City clinic (quoted in Patton 1986a).

Conclusion

Despite claims to the contrary from SBC proponents and staff members, the evidence clearly shows that even if the school clinic does not itself perform abortions, the staff will use their presence within the school to channel pregnant girls to abortion mills either through direct or indirect referrals. Moreover, if abortion pills, such as RU 486, become legal in the United States and distributed through the family-planning clinic network, there would be little to stop school clinics from becoming centers for mass abortion.

Possible Remedies

The most effective way to prevent school clinics from promoting abortion is to not open them on campus. If that is not feasible, the abortion issue can only be neutralized by cutting off the school clinics' links to any organization or agency that performs, counsels, or refers for abortions. SBC supporters will fiercely fight any restrictions on their operations, and if they cannot run it unhampered they may even withdraw support for a clinic at least temporarily until the environment changes. The specific terms of legislation or regulations to accomplish this goal will naturally be different for each local school district, or county, or state.

CHAPTER THREE

PRO-ABORTION AGENDA OF CLINIC PROMOTERS

J udging from the tenor of the public debate about SBCs, many decision-makers are apparently under the erroneous impression that the research studies promoting government support for school clinics come from neutral sources, who have no stake in the outcome. Nothing could be further from the truth.

As we shall see in this chapter, the Planned Parenthood Federation, its research arm—the Alan Guttmacher Institute—the Center for Population Options, and several major foundations that are orchestrating the current nationwide campaign to establish SBCs, have a long history of pro-abortion advocacy. Since they are not disinterested and objective parties, their "experts," statistics, pseudo-scientific analysis, and recommendations should be judged accordingly. Unfortunately, they have already had a major influence on the public-policy debate over SBCs.

Planned Parenthood Federation of America

Promoting School-Based Clinics

Since mid-1985, the Planned Parenthood Federation of America, the largest, wealthiest, and most prestigious of the non-profit organizations promoting school clinics, has mobilized all of its considerable public relations and lobbying forces behind an effort to create a national movement to solve the "epidemic of teenage pregnancy." The Federation proudly considers that its "mission is to serve as the nation's foremost agent of social change in area of reproductive health and well being," and it strongly backs the school-based clinic movement because it advances Planned Parenthood's goals (Planned Parenthood 1975, 5; Curry 1986). In addition to being active on a national level, Planned Parenthood's affiliates and state-level lobbying offices have been particularly vigorous supporters of local initiatives to set up SBCs in, for example, Michigan, Pennsylvania, and Washington, D.C. (Muskegon Area Planned Parenthood 1985a; McNamara 1986; Zlatos 1986, B1; Allegar 1985).

The Federation's leaders have been very adept at using advertising, lobbying, and publicity to move their key issues to the top of the stack in Congress and state legislatures where they receive priority attention. For example, Planned Parenthood uses the media to manufacture what appears to be a consensus behind the direction that it wants public policy to go. A favorite ploy recently has been to commission a carefully crafted public opinion poll and then manipulate the media coverage of the announcement of the results. This arrangement gives the impression that the public supports the Federation's agenda. Let's take two examples.

Sixty-seven percent of respondents to a national Harris poll in August 1985 commissioned by the Planned Parenthood Federation favored "requiring public schools to establish *links* with family planning clinics" (Harris 1985, 40; emphasis added). However, the Federation's president, Faye Wattleton, transformed those results into something quite different. She told a reporter in August 1986 that the poll revealed that "67 percent of the respondents favored *school-based* health clinics that offer family planning services" (emphasis added; Callen 1986). Wattleton should have pointed out that *linking* a clinic with a school is *not the same* as actually *basing* one inside.

A similar manipulation took place in December 1986 when the Planned Parenthood Federation published the results of a nationwide Harris poll of teenagers' views on sex, pregnancy, and birth control. A press report gave the impression that a majority of the teens polled favored school-based clinics (*OB. GYN. News* 1987, 2). Actually, forty-nine percent—a solid majority—of the teens who answered the question about "school-linked clinics" said that the clinics should be located "somewhere else" instead of "inside the schools" or "close to the schools" (Harris 1986, 71) Only twelve percent of the teens favored placing clinics "inside the schools," while twenty-eight percent supported placing clinics "close to the schools." (Eleven percent refused to answer the question.)

Supporting Unrestricted Abortion

Planned Parenthood is so effective an advocate for SBCs because of its reputation as a disinterested health-care provider and educator. Since the Federation downplays its status as an abortion provider and lobbyist, except among selected groups of citizens whom it hopes to enlist as contributors to its cause, many members of the public remain unaware of the organization's rock-hard opposition to any restrictions on the abortion liberty. Moreover, seldom mentions Planned Parenthood's connection with abortion.

The evidence demonstrating the Federation's abortion advocacy is overwhelming. Planned Parenthood operates the nation's largest chain of abortion facilities and is the leading promoter of abortion in the United States. A telephone survey of all Planned Parenthood affiliates in July 1987 revealed that 48 affiliates in 27 states operated sixty separate abortion chambers (Glasow 1987a, 6). Abortion statistics published in the Federation's *Service Report* in October 1987 (describing its 1986 operations) revealed that the organization's affiliates were responsible for a total of 191,487 abortions in 1986 (Planned Parenthood 1987b, 9). Its affiliates were directly involved in over 10% of the estimated 1.6 million abortions performed nationwide during 1986. Forty-eight Planned Parenthood affiliates performed 98,638 abortions in 1986, and the Federation's 183 affiliates referred another 92,849 pregnant women and girls to abortionists that year.

The Planned Parenthood Federation has been an outspoken and vigorous supporter of abortion for almost two decades. In 1969, the Federation adopted a policy favoring radical changes in law to give women virtually unrestricted access to abortion and rapidly built the nation's most extensive abortion referral network (Nancy Hicks 1969, 17; Langmyhr 1971, 1190). Since 1978, under the leadership of a militant pro-abortion faction, the Federation has spent millions of dollars on a lobbying, litigation, fundraising, and advertising campaign to defend abortion-on-demand and defeat any type of law promoting notification or consent of parents before their daughter obtains an abortion (Wattleton 1982; Planned Parenthood 1987a, 18-21).

Planned Parenthood's Alan Guttmacher Institute Promotes "Social Change"

Special Affiliate Status

Planned Parenthood has been especially successful in establishing its research affiliate, the Alan Guttmacher Institute, as an authoritative and seemingly "objective" spokesman and analyst in the debate over SBCs.

Planned Parenthood founded the Guttmacher Institute in June 1968 as the Center for Family Planning Program Development. Although separately incorporated since 1977, the Institute has interlocking boards of directors with the Federation and is still heavily supported financially by the Federation as its "special research affiliate." For example, Planned Parenthood gave $445,000 to the Institute in 1983, the last year for which information is available. The remainder of the Institute's support comes from federal contracts, donations, and grants from foundations that share Planned Parenthood's agenda (Planned Parenthood 1983; Alan Guttmacher Institute 1985).

Propaganda Disguised As Objective Research

The Guttmacher Institute's research studies published in its bimonthly magazine, *Family Planning Perspectives*, have provided much of the impetus for the enormously successful current campaign promoting school-based clinics as an effective "solution" to the so-called "epidemic" of teen pregnancy.

One could question the objectivity of this periodical because the publisher is so heavily underwritten financially by an advocacy organization. Moreover, the fact that *Perspectives* serves primarily as a propaganda vehicle and not a legitimate social science research publication is evident from the consistent advocacy positions taken in its articles and editorials. For example, since the early 1970s, the Institute's researchers have regularly published an authoritative survey on the availability of abortions nationwide which pinpointed for prospective abortionists where they could find more "clients." The authors consistently decried the fact that more abortions were not being done. For example, in 1976, they estimated that the "unmet need" for abortions was between 150,000 and 650,000 (Alan Guttmacher Institute 1976, 13 and 16).

According to the Guttmacher Institute's 1985 *Annual Report*, the staff members pride themselves on "fostering social change through generation and application of policy-relevant information." The "year's most noteworthy achievement," explained the report, was the publication of a multinational study in the March/April 1985 issue of *Perspectives* calling for more federal and state spending on teen pregnancy prevention programs. Anyone reading newspaper clippings from around the country could not help but agree with the Institute staff's assessment of their article's "far-reaching and catalytic" impact (Alan Guttmacher Institute 1985, 9).

For example, this multinational study provided a major stimulus for a significant influx of tens of millions of dollars in foundation grants to SBCs and other pro-abortion organizations. According to an article in the *New York Times* May 19, 1986, "[f]oundation spokesman said their increased attention to this field, particularly adolescent pregnancy, stemmed in part" from the Guttmacher Institute's article published the previous year (Teltsch 1986, A15). "'Now, new ideas about adolescent pregnancy such as school-

based clinics and broader sex-education curriculum have captured the foundations' attention,' said Joy Dryfoos, a consultant to both the Rockefeller and
Carnegie foundations," reported the *Times*. Despite many serious methodological deficiencies, the study is still widely cited by policymakers to justify
initiating major new teen pregnancy prevention programs along the lines
recommended in the report. (Appendix Two provides a detailed critique of
this study.)

The Guttmacher Institute's influence did not end there. During 1985 and
1986, *Family Planning Perspectives* published three of the most widely quoted
articles extolling the virtues of SBCs: Joy Dryfoos' analysis of the status of
school clinics (March 1985), Asta Kenney's report on the October 1985
annual SBC conference (January 1986), and Laurie Zabin's article describing
the Baltimore clinic program (July 1986) (Dryfoos 1985b; Kenney 1986a;
Zabin et al. 1986).

Zabin's influential study will be discussed in more detail in Chapter Five,
but it is important to note here that news articles fail to point out that she
could hardly act as a disinterested, objective analyst of SBCs because of her
close association with both Planned Parenthood and the Guttmacher Institute
for the past two decades. During the 1960s, she served two years as the
president of Planned Parenthood's Maryland affiliate, held five committee
chairmanships on the national Planned Parenthood board, and currently
serves as both the chairman of the board of the Guttmacher Institute and a
member of the national board of the Planned Parenthood Federation
(Henderson 1987). Zabin acquired her special celebrity status through her
association with Johns Hopkins University and directorship of a school-
clinic operated in Baltimore for twenty-eight months from 1981 through
1984.[1]

Alan Guttmacher Institute Influences National Academy Study

The pervasive influence of the Guttmacher Institute's experts on the public-
policy debate over SBCs was especially evident in December 1986 when the
National Research Council (NRC) of the prestigious National Academy of
Sciences published a "scientific" analysis of the teen pregnancy problem and
suggested specific solutions to ameliorate it. The Institute's fingerprints are all
over the book titled *Risking The Future: Adolescent Sexuality, Pregnancy,
and Childbearing*, written by the Council's Panel on Adolescent Pregnancy
and Childbearing (Hayes 1987).

Three NRC panel members have been closely associated with the Institute. Joy Dryfoos, currently a consultant for the Carnegie Foundation and a widely quoted national authority on SBCs, served during the early 1970s as the Institute's director of planning (Sullivan, Tietze and Dryfoos 1977, 116). Frank Furstenberg, a sociologist at the University of Pennsylvania, published several articles in *Family Planning Perspectives* and co-edited a book of essays that had previously appeared in *Perspectives* (Furstenberg 1981). And panelist Jacqueline D. Forrest is the Institute's current director of research. Her writings are also widely cited in the book (Hayes 1987, 154, 155, 157, 159, 302).

Throughout *Risking The Future*, the NRC panel relied heavily on the Guttmacher's Institute's publications and research. For example, most of the information in the section on abortion came from articles published in *Family Planning Perspectives*. The panel also explicitly adopted the Planned Parenthood-Guttmacher Institute policy "line" on several key issues, including the conclusion that state laws requiring parental notice and consent would harm, rather than help, a minor girl. This became the basis for the panel's most controversial recommendation that minors should have unrestricted access to confidential, government-funded abortions (Hayes 1987, 112-115, 193-194, 278-279).

In summary, Alan Guttmacher Institute and the Planned Parenthood Federation of America are a formidable pair of pro-abortion advocates for SBCs. Both have excellent access to foundation funding and enjoy especially good press. On the one hand, Planned Parenthood brings to the movement its unparalleled nationwide outreach through its affiliates, its lobbying offices in Washington, D.C. and many state capitals, and its experience in building coalitions to achieve its legislative goals. On the other hand, the Guttmacher Institute's assets in the struggle to create public sentiment for SBCs include its solid (if undeserved) reputation as a source for reliable statistics and analysis on reproductive health issues, and its ability to generate impressive publications supporting its public-policy objectives.

Center for Population Options

Promoting School Clinics

The third pro-abortion organization with a pivotal role in the pro-SBC movement has the enigmatic name of the Center for Population Options. By devoting almost all of its resources to promoting SBCs, the Center has exercised a major influence on clinic development.

The Center for Population Options carved out a unique niche for itself by opening the first national Support Center for School-Based Clinics in April

1985 (Lovick and Wesson 1986, 19). With two project offices in Houston and Washington, D.C., the Support Center has become the focal point and clearinghouse for gathering and sharing information among SBC advocates.

The Support Center's staff offers technical assistance through a network of consultants, holds training seminars and conferences to train clinic staff and community leaders, and publishes materials to foster the establishment of clinics. The Center for Population Options' media outreach office in Los Angeles seeks to influence television productions handling teen-pregnancy issues.

The central role of the SBC Support Center in Houston in boosting school clinics was evident from the statistics recited by the director, Sharon R. Lovick, in the closing speech at the SBC national conference held in October 1986 (Lovick 1986). A tabulation of activities over the previous twelve months indicated that the center had "logged almost 1,700 individual requests for information," she said, and the staff followed up about 40% of them with written answers or materials. In addition, Lovick reported that staff members from the Houston and Washington offices provided technical assistance in thirty different states and had given twenty-eight major presentations to over 3,500 people during the year.

Apparently, the pace has not slackened at all. The February 16, 1987 issue of Newsweek quoted Center staff member Wanda Wesson as saying "that the center gets about 100 requests for help a month from schools wanting to begin new projects" (Kantrowitz 1987, 58).

Another illustration of the Center for Population Options' impact was a comment at a national conference on adolescent pregnancy prevention in March 1987 made by David Gurule, program manager of the Adolescent Health Program, Oregon State Health Division, who played a pivotal role establishing school-based clinics throughout his state. During the process of setting up the facilities, he called Sharon Lovick every day for advice and moral support (Gurule 1987).

Moreover, the Center for Population Options' sponsorship of four annual national conferences on SBCs—in Houston in 1984, Chicago in 1985, Denver in 1986, and Kansas City, Missouri in 1987—provided an especially important impetus to the growth of SBCs. The meetings offer SBC staff members and advocates an opportunity to exchange information through both formal presentations and informal gatherings, and to build a common sense of purpose, which gives the movement momentum.

In addition to the office in Houston run by Sharon Lovick, who formerly directed a SBC in that city, staff members in the Center for Population Option's Washington headquarters also work on SBCs. The Houston branch handles training and technical assistance, while policy information and assistance questions are directed primarily to the director of public policy in Washington, D.C. (Center for Pop. Options 1986d, page ii).

Another Center staff member based in Washington, Douglas Kirby, director of research, wrote the widely quoted booklet describing the results of the first SBC conference in Houston. Published in April 1985, "School-Based Health Clinics: An Emerging Approach to Improving Adolescent Health and Addressing Teenage Pregnancy" ranks with the three Guttmacher Institute's articles publications on SBCs mentioned above as one of the most thorough surveys of the goals and methods of operation of school clinics (Kirby 1985).

Two other Center for Population Options' publications are worth mentioning. A quarterly newsletter, "Clinic News," informs advocates about program developments, legislation, and new resources. In October 1986, the Center published a comprehensive ninety-eight-page manual on how to start and operate a SBC, which will undoubtedly be widely used as the SBC movement grows (Hadley 1986).

Now that we have seen how the Center for Population Options plays a key role in the SBC movement, we let us turn to an analysis of its stance on abortion.

Pro-Abortion Advocacy

The Center for Population Options may not be as well known for pro-abortion advocacy as some other organizations such as the Planned Parenthood Federation and the Guttmacher Institute; but, its history and public-policy statements surely show that the organization is firmly against any pro-life initiatives and in favor of unrestricted abortion-on-demand.

Links to Population Institute

The Center for Population Options was formed in 1980 as an offshoot of the Population Institute in order to focus exclusively on teen pregnancy, and the progeny adopted its parent organization's ideological position supporting abortion-on-demand.

The Population Institute has been a long-time supporter of abortion in foreign countries, and its recent activities provide an excellent measure of its leadership's strong committment to the issue. During the last two years, the Institute moved into the headlines through its aggressive lobbying and advertising campaign to restore U.S. funding for organizations that support coerced abortion overseas (Johnson 1986, 1).

Opposition to Pro-Life Legislative Initiatives

Soon after being established, the Center for Population Options (CPO) took an unequivocal public position in 1981 against two major legislative measures aimed at restricting abortion, the Human Life Bill (Senate Bill 158) and the Human Life Federalism Amendment (Senate Joint Resolution 110, later known in an amended form as the Hatch/Eagleton Amendment). "CPO's Board of Directors supports access to safe and legal abortion for Americans of all ages," stated the organization's testimony in June to the U.S. Senate Subcommittee on Separation of Powers, "and has placed a priority on programs that seek to guarantee such access" (U.S. Congress. Senate 1982a, 158). Six months later in December, Judith Senderowitz, the organization's executive director, submitted testimony to the U.S. Senate Subcommittee on the Constitution stating that "CPO opposes all constitutional amendments designed to nullify the Supreme Court's *Roe v. Wade* decision" (U.S. Congress. Senate 1983, 36).

In January 1983, the tenth anniversary of the Court's ruling, the Center for Population Options joined other leading pro-abortion organizations at a press conference in Washington, D.C. to announce a "new, aggressive" campaign "to roll back local, state or federal laws" that attempt to restrict abortion in any way (Pilpel 1983). In the Center's press statement prepared for the event, Senderowitz proclaimed that "Today we celebrate a vital Supreme Court decision, *Roe v. Wade*, which upholds a woman's right to choose an abortion (Center for Pop. Options 1983).

Working On Teenagers

The Center for Population Options' pro-abortion position has also been apparent during the last two years in its efforts to thwart right-to-life educational efforts among teenagers. The organization's *Annual Report 1984-1985* cited a "disturbing" fact: "a major decline (from 74% to 54%) over the past decade or so in the adolescent support for legal abortion" (Center for Pop. Options 1985, 9). Research commissioned by the Center had disclosed, stated the report, "evidence that anti-abortion publicity effectively reaches teenagers," and that it "may influence both their political attitudes and their practical decisions."

In August 1986, the Center conducted a joint survey with Catholics for a Free Choice (a pro-abortion lobbying and educational organization of dissident, nominal Catholics) to assess how pro-lifers reached teenagers so effectively (Kissling and Senderowitz 1986). According to the Center's *Annual*

Report 1986-1987, they "found a disturbing lack of pro-choice [that is, pro-abortion] educational efforts and informational materials relevant to teens" (Center for Pop. Options 1987a, 10).

Funding from Pro-abortion Foundations

One final example of the Center for Population Options' link to the pro-abortion cause is its heavy reliance on income from foundations with long records of supporting organizations which promote abortion overseas and fight pro-life legislative initiatives. In 1984 and 1985, for example, the Center received a total of $600,000 in grants from five sources: the Hewlett Foundation ($225,000), the Robert Sterling Clark Foundation ($30,000), the William T. Grant Foundation ($225,000), the Packard Foundation ($70,000), and the Noyes Foundation ($50,000) (Hewlett Foundation 1985; Foundation Center 1986a, 455-56 and 54, 57; Foundation Center 1986b, 27; Foundation Center 1986c, 35; Foundation Center 1987a, 22).

Foundations Support SBCs, Foster Abortion

Let us now examine the activities of the clinic advocates' silent partners—the private foundations—which have had a much less public role. These institutions provide essential financial and administrative assistance—if not the primary impetus in some cities—for opening school clinics.

During the last half century, foundations have performed many valuable services to advance the public welfare; however, the very features of foundations that have contributed to that success—control of huge financial resources, and isolation of a small self-perpetuating board of directors from public accountability—also endow them with enormous destructive power. And that unfortunately is what is presently occurring as foundations crusade for school clinics.

Like the movement to legalize abortion, the pro-SBC movement was started and is being sustained by the steady influx of millions of dollars from foundations. It would be fair to say that school-based clinics would not exist without their support.

Since most foundations usually do not provide a detailed explanation of the reasons behind their grants to SBCs—and none have clearly linked their giving to advocacy of abortion—we must draw inferences. However, there is the additional fact that the foundations providing the bulk of the money to SBCs have also supported pro-abortion causes in the past, as we shall see.

This section may also make readers aware of the disproportionate impact that a small group of foundation officers and their cronies have had on shaping the whole public debate over SBCs because of the amounts of money that they donate. Judging from the evidence here, the cliché "money is power" seems true.

Millions of Dollars Pour Into Clinics

According to the Center for Population Options' "SBC Update" published in October 1986, private foundations provided a striking 31% of the total funding for the SBCs currently in operation (Lovick and Wesson 1986, 13). No dollar figure was given, but the amount would certainly total several million dollars per year nationwide. The two other sources of private funds only provided a total of 5%. (Government sources provided the other 64%.) The brief report did not provide any more details about which foundations were involved.

In addition to supporting clinics directly, foundation grants to organizations such as the Center for Population Options and the Children's Defense Fund have provided the impetus for both publicity and research to create wide-spread public concern about the so-called "epidemic of teenage pregnancy." School clinics are offered as one of the best solutions. At the same time that momentum is being generated at the grassroots level, foundation money supports efforts to influence legislators through lobbying and production of impressive materials with the pro-SBC point of view.

Foundation Money Starts Clinics In Chicago

The controversy over two school-based clinics in Chicago offers one of the best examples of the tremendous influence that foundations may exercise on the public-policy process. In 1982, Irving B. Harris, of the Harris Foundation and Pittway Charitable Corporation, arranged with Gregory Coler, then director of the Illinois Department of Children and Family Services (and now director of the Department of Public Aid), to establish a public-private partnership, named the Ounce of Prevention Fund (Ounce of Prevention Fund 1985). Matching grants of $400,000 from the Pittway and the state launched the Fund, which subsequently received funding from the Commonwealth Fund, the Robert Wood Johnson Foundation, and the Joyce Foundation.

In October 1985, the Ounce of Prevention Fund co-sponsored the second annual national SBC conference where it proudly showcased its newly opened DuSable Clinic on Chicago's south side. The organization opened its second clinic in August 1986 at Orr Community Academy, another public high school (Banas 1986, 1).

The Ounce of Prevention Fund now serves as the conduit for the hundreds of thousands of dollars of state and private operating funds to both the DuSable and Orr clinics. According to the *New York Times*, DuSable receives half of its $225,000 annual income from the Illinois Department of Public Aid and the remainder from a coalition of private foundations. Both clinics have received an eight-year committment of support; thereafter, they will almost certainly need to find public funding. In view of this, we can estimate that the minimum amount of foundation grants for just those two clinics over that period will be $1 million (Associated Press 1986, A24).

Since the Fund is a private organization, it insulates the clinics from both public scrutiny and public pressure. For example, when the controversy exploded in September 1985 over the DuSable clinic, having a professional staff who could work full-time with the media enabled the Fund to contour the debate well enough to turn it to their advantage, according to a senior staff member (Carter 1986).

Pro-Abortion Foundations Promote School Clinics

Two other notable examples from the ranks of the nation's largest foundations illustrates the magnitude of the resources that have poured into the SBC movement.

Ford Foundation

The Ford Foundation, the nation's wealthiest philanthropic organization, moved into the teen-pregnancy issue in the late 1970s, and the organization has a long record of supporting abortion extending back to the 1960s. For example, in February 1984 the foundation gave a $276,400, five-year grant to the Population Council for development of the abortion pill, RU-486 (Foundation Center 1985, 331). A Ford grant of $50,000 in June 1985 to the Catholics for a Free Choice, a pro-abortion lobbying and educational group, aimed to assist the distribution of its publications "related to abortion" (Foundation Center 1986a, 361).

Marilyn Steele, a program officer with the Mott Foundation, reported in the spring 1986 issue of *Planned Parenthood Review* that between 1982 and 1985 the Ford Foundation "had committed almost $8 million to teen-age pregnancy prevention programs." (Steele 1986, 12) For example, in October

1984, the foundation announced a two-and-a-half year, $104,000 grant to the Center for Population Options to fund a workshop for clinic administrators and to evaluate school-based clinics. As a major supporter of the NRC panel's research on teen pregnancy published as *Risking The Future*, the Ford Foundation ensured that its point of view would be recognized in that important study, which strongly advocated guaranteeing a government-funded abortion to any pregnant teen who wants one.

Carnegie Corporation

On May 16, 1986, the *New York Times* reported that the Carnegie Corporation of New York, a philanthropic foundation with over $565 million in assets, had committed to spending $4 million over the next two years to prevent pregnancies among adolescents (Teltsch 1986, A15). The Center for Population Options was one beneficiary of that program, according to Carnegie's 1985 annual report, as the recipient of a two-year grant of $180,000 to "influence television and Hollywood producers on adolescent sexuality and pregnancy" (Carnegie 1985, 38). Carnegie's general teen initiative and the Center for Population Options' grant should not be a surprise since the foundation had employed CPO's chairman of the board, Joy Dryfoos, as a consultant to study adolescent pregnancy issues.

In December 1984, the Carnegie Corporation announced a three-year grant of $1 million to the Children's Defense Fund's (CDF) nationwide multimedia campaign on adolescent pregnancy, including promotion of SBCs. CDF is certainly not in the same class of pro-abortion crusaders as Planned Parenthood and the Center for Population Options, but the fact remains that CDF is strongly promoting establishment of school-based clinics without any restrictions on abortion counseling and referrals.

The Children's Defense Fund's articulate and influential president, Marion Wright Edelman, has publicly declared that her organization is neutral on the abortion issue (Children's Defense Fund 1987a, 4); however, in 1979 CDF lobbied diligently against passage of an anti-abortion amendment to the federal Child Health Assurance Program (known as CHAP). The amendment was aimed at preventing federal funds from being spent for abortions in a proposed expansion of the health screening program (Children's Defense Fund 1979, 5). Apparently, the organization has not taken any other public stances on abortion-related legislation since then.

In January 1983, the Children's Defense Fund initiated a well-coordinated, multi-phase media campaign to focus national public attention on the problem of teen pregnancy, with special emphasis on the Black community. In addition to a comprehensive print, television and radio effort, the organization operates an Adolescent Pregnancy Prevention Clearinghouse and publishes a series of pamphlets on relevant issues (Childrens' Defense Fund 1987a, 2).

The print advertising effort which premiered in 1986 sought to alert adults to the problem of teenage pregnancy and mobilize them into action in their own community (Children's Defense Fund 1987b). The ads intentionally avoid offering solutions, which sets the stage very nicely for Planned Parenthood and the other SBC proponents to follow up with their pro-abortion agenda.

The print and transit ads in phase two directed at teenagers are even more troubling from a right-to-life perspective. According to the campaign promotional literature, the objective was to link "teenage parenting with a concept of personal loss understandable to teens" (Children's Defense Fund 1987b). When that professional jargon was translated into ad copy, the resulting product was not as benign as it may have started out. Two assumptions lurk behind all of the ads. First, the campaign ignores adoption as a option for a pregnant teenager. The ads assume that the pregnant teenager will decide to keep her baby rather than give it up for adoption. The second assumption is even more fatalistic: a teenager who decides to keep her baby will find her life in shambles.

The result of this overly simplistic and one-sided approach is that the ads carry a strong anti-life message. The print campaign depict grim, young mothers with unattractive babies with words stating that babies create problems. Although the ads were evidently aimed at convincing teens not to get pregnant, an equally apparent message would unfortunately be to abort rather than bring another "unwelcome and burdensome" child into the world. Teens already have the second highest abortion rate of any age group, and they do not need additional influences in that direction.

Robert Wood Johnson Foundation

One organization strongly supporting SBCs that is in class by itself is the Robert Wood Johnson Foundation, the nation's largest philanthropy devoted to health. No other foundation comes near equaling the approximately $40 million that it pours into health research and medical care yearly. Although the foundation does not have an overtly pro-abortion agenda, it extends a strong influence in helping establish and operate more clinics without any restrictions on the SBC's promotion of abortion.

In April 1986, the Johnson Foundation announced that its School-Based Adolescent Health Care Program would grant $16.8 million over the next six years to twenty communities of more than 100,000 people to establish clinics in schools (Robert Wood Johnson 1986a; 1986b, 3 and 6). Each grant could total up to $600,000 over the six-year period. According to the "Guidelines for Grant Applications," clinics receiving funds must offer a "comprehensive range of services", including "referral and follow-up for . . . pregnancy" (i.e. abortion counseling and referrals). According to a report in the *New York Times*, "each community is to decide if contraceptives or abortion will be provided" (Teltsch 1986, A15).

However, in trying to evaluate the meaning and possible motives behind this rather vague wording, one should realize that this current SBC initiative grew out of a five-year demonstration project conducted from 1978 through 1983 in eight medically underserved locations and eighteen schools (Robert Wood Johnson 1985, 3).

On one hand, one might think that the foundation's officers had benign objectives, not recognizing the SBCs' connection to abortion referrals and education. After all, the apparent impetus for offering grants for a broad-based health care system grew out of the experience in a pilot school-based project in the late 1970s and early 1980s which allegedly showed that comprehensive health care improved students' health and helped them to learn more.

On the other hand, the previous experimental projects were quite different than the proposed SBCs in two highly important respects. First, they were operated only by school nurses rather than the much larger staff utilized in school clinics. Second, the schools which participated in the pilot project did not include abortion counseling and referrals. Therefore, the foundation staff must certainly realize that requiring prospective grantees to offer those services certainly will raise questions about what their real objectives are.

Two final points are worth noting because they provide an indication of the direction that the foundation is going. First, grants from Robert Wood Johnson and several other philanthropies funded a pilot counseling and health screening program for teenagers in the South Bronx named the "Hub" (Teltsch 1986, A15). The center was jointly operated by Bronx-Lebanon Hospital and Planned Parenthood of New York City and was located in the same building with one of PP's abortion chambers. Second, one of senior officials in the foundation responsible for the SBC program is Terrance Keenan, vice president for special programs. He will be quoted in Chapter Six praising the virtues of using outside organizations to operate clinics in order to give the clinic staff more latitude in determining what services that they could offer, which translates into more abortion counseling and referrals.

In addition to actually funding clinics in twenty cities, the Robert Wood Johnson program had an additional powerful effect which may in the long run turn out to be more important. The announcement of the multi-million dollar SBC sweepstakes initiated a nationwide scramble to get a piece of the pie. Suddenly school board members and city fathers (and mothers) who probably would not have seriously considered opening a clinic started listening to Planned Parenthood and other SBC proponents who had plans already drafted for discussion and approval (Kollars 1986, A1; Lou Cook 1987, 28; Madison 1986, 1).

Over eighty agencies filed applications, and in June 1987 the foundation announced the first series of ten grantees (for thirteen clinics in nine cities). A second round of grants to seven agencies (for nine clinics in seven cities) was made public in July 1987 (Center for Pop. Options 1987b, 1).

Many cities could not meet the program's requirements and did not get applications for the Johnson Foundation grants. But in some cases the momentum for establishing SBCs persisted because of continued publicity and interest by public officials (i.e. Lou Cook 1987, 28).

In summary, the best that can be said of the Children's Defense Fund and the Robert Wood Johnson Foundation is that they are unwitting allies to the mainstream SBC proponents such as Planned Parenthood and the Center for Population Options who have a pro-abortion agenda. At worst, the Defense Fund and the Johnson Foundation are willing accomplices in a well-coordinated campaign to establish SBCs to reduce teen births by increasing abortions.

Conclusion

After this review of the advocacy track record of the Planned Parenthood Federation of America and its allies on a variety of legislative, media, and educational fronts, the reader may be surprised that these agencies have been able to, on the one hand, lobby effectively for opening school clinics, yet on the other hand, maintain an unreserved reputation of being "objective" comentators. This situation is no surprise for veteran right-to-life supporters, but just a replay of a bad experience in the late 1960s and early 1970s when the same organizations used the identical techniques to legalize abortion.

SBC proponents are extremely savvy with entree into the media elites and the highest ranks of the medical-scientific establishment. Bankrolled by powerful foundations and armed with pseudo-scientific research studies, the Planned Parenthood Federation and its allies have successfully orchestrated a media blitz that formulated the terms of the public debate over teen pregnancies.

This chapter has answered the questions: who are the people behind the push for SBCs? and what did they do in the past? The next chapter identifies what they expect to gain in the future if SBCs are established.

CHAPTER FOUR

ENORMOUS STAKES FOR SCHOOL-BASED CLINIC PROPONENTS

A ll too readily, the public, policymakers and the media accept at face value the pronouncements of SBC advocates without recognizing the enormous financial and ideological stake in the clinic debate for proponents. On one hand, the Planned Parenthood Federation and its allies, such as the Center for Population Options, could achieve two long-standing ideological goals. On the other hand, Planned Parenthood and the Alan Guttmacher Institute could increase their income and enhance their prospects for long-term stability. Naturally, the proponents conceal these self-serving motives from the public.

Using Teens to Attain Ideological Goals

Pressuring Teens Into The Clinics

First, widespread establishment of SBCs would achieve a major objective of the pro-abortion lobby, one that extends back over two decades: to pressure teenagers into changing their behavior. Operating a *school*-based facility offers unique advantages over the previous *community*-based clinic, observed Douglas Kirby in his authoritative summary of SBCs' policies and activities. SBC staff members "claim that the three most important reasons why school clinics work," Kirby said, "are location, location, and location" (Kirby 1985, 13).

Since so much of the public debate revolves around the implications of putting clinics *inside* the schools, we will examine in detail what the SBC proponents see as the three most attractive features of being located in the school, reasons which are closely linked: better proximity to students, which increases the capability to modify the teenagers' behavior, and with greater confidentiality. As we shall see in later chapters, from the opponents' point of view, these "advantages" enable Planned Parenthood and its allies to invade teenagers' lives more easily, coerce more students into obtaining more abortions, and cut out parents even further from crucially important decisions in their children's lives.

Daily Contact

The first advantage of SBCs, according to proponents, is that it means advocates will be much closer to where teens are every day. During the last decade and a half, Planned Parenthood and its pro-abortion allies have continually bemoaned their inability to attract large enough numbers of teenagers into their clinics (Herceg-Baron 1986, 61; Haffner 1986; Jones 1985, 60-61; Jones 1986, 236-238; Hayes 1987, 157). Since they had to wait passively for the teens to come to them, the clinics developed methods, which include teen theatre, sending sex educators into the schools, advertising in school publications, and peer counselors, to infiltrate their messages into the high schools (Planned Parenthood 1986b, 17-36).

School-based clinics offer an unprecedented opportunity for virtually unlimited access to teens since clinicians are located where teens are required by law to be every day. The close proximity allows the staff to become part of the school environment where they can influence students both inside and outside of the clinic. For example, Dr. Leroy Taylor, a dentist who leads the health staff of the West Dallas High School clinic, explained to a *Washington Post* reporter, "We try not to just see them in the examining room" (Fisher 1987, A8). He takes two other staff members "to the gym every week to shoot hoops with students," reported thè *Post*. Likewise, the nurse-practitioner in the SBC operated by Planned Parenthood in Muskegon, Michigan explained in a *Newsweek* story published on February 16, 1987 that "[i]n the schools, you have a beautiful system for follow-up because the nurse in a school has access to kids in a hallway to say, 'How's it going?'" (Kantrowitz 1987, 57).

Using School Authority

In addition to being close to the students, the staff of a school-based facility has the second advantage of having authority and control over the teenagers. Placing the clinic inside of the school sends a not-so-subtle message to the teens that the school is legitimizing the clinic's programs. There are several reasons to fear that in an effort to force teens to modify their behavior, the operators such as Planned Parenthood could become even more coercive than they already are in their non-school facilities.

One reason is that, given the confidentiality surrounding the clinics' operations, there is little control over what the staff does behind the closed doors. As described in Chapter Six, in order to prevent parents and school authorities from learning what services are provided to the students, the SBC may maintain two sets of records on each student who visits the clinic—one set for parents and officials to see, and the other with information the staff wants to keep hidden.

Another reason to oppose opening SBCs is that the present clinics use the school's authority to invade the students' privacy and push them around in ways that would be unthinkable were they adults. According to Douglas Kirby, "many of the [SBC] programs include discussion of sexual activity as part of the first visit during the routine health assessment of all clients, male and female." In other words, every student who comes to a clinic obstensibly for other reasons is subjected to a thorough interrogation—not Kirby's words, naturally—about her or his "sexual behavior and birth control" (Kirby 1985, 8 and 13).

Ensuring "Compliance"

Moreover, successful school-based programs, observed Kirby, "typically make a considerable effort to follow-up on services, thus ensuring client *compliance*" (emphasis added; Kirby 1985, 13). "The school clinic pulls students out of class for appointments," he said, "just as a school nurse would." A staff member of a SBC in Kansas City, Missouri gave an example of this aggressive attitude at the national SBC conference in Chicago in 1985 when she described how "if they don't show up, we go get them" (Kaegi 1985, 4). "That's one of the advantages," she explained, "of being in the school."

Possible Coercion

The most disturbing aspect of the attitude of the SBC proponent toward modifying the behavior of teenagers is the possibility that "compliance" may soon slip into coercion. Joy Dryfoos, one of the most active and influential clinic promoters, has seriously suggested a rationale for clinics to abandon any appearance of offering "non-directive" counseling. She recommended ways by which the clinics can *compel* adolescents to adopt the pattern of behavior favored by the clinic staff.

In an editorial published in January 1985 in the *Journal of the American Public Health Association*, the nation's largest association of health professionals, she drew a parallel between the ability of schools to force teenagers to do homework and what their health clinics *could* be doing along the same line (Dryfoos 1985a, 13). In her view, clinics should drop their current "non-coercive" policies with some teens and take a harder line by insisting that they "comply with a regimen." Another way of describing this approach, explained Dryfoos to a group of journalists in May 1986, is "authoritative guidance," which will require that clinic personnel take "a much more directive approach to young people" (Dryfoos 1986b, 10).

Dryfoos' promotion of this coercive policy is particularly worrisome since she also preaches to clinic staffers that if they can arrange for outside agencies to operate the clinics, "then you can do all kinds of things in schools that you never dreamed of" (quoted in Coughlan 1987b). One does not need a very active imagination to see where that could lead.

Cutting Out Parents

In addition to the advantages of being close to the students and having the authority to pull them into the clinic, placing the clinic inside of the school virtually guarantees that Planned Parenthood and its allies can provide "medical treatment" to teens without parental knowledge or consent. The clinic's staff can follow up on students through the school's communication network, which avoids contacting the teenagers at home.

The "relative effectiveness of the school-based clinics is clearly related to the ease with which the young people can be followed up without endangering the confidentiality of the relationship," stated Dr. Laura Edwards, who started the St. Paul school clinic (Edwards et al. 1980, 12). In programs outside of the school, she stated, "it is often difficult to follow adolescent clinic patients who have not informed their parents about their participating, but in the school program, the young people can be reached *without communications to the home*" (emphasis added).

SBCs As Surrogate Parents?

SBC proponents come naturally to using such blatant underhanded methods because of an almost missionary zeal to act as stand-in parents. SBC staffers do not perceive a teenager as part of a family unit, but quite separate from her or his parents. Employing what could be called a "public-health" point of view, SBCs regard a teenager as an independent patient capable of giving informed consent to receive reproductive health services without parental knowledge and consent.

During the *Parents: Consent and Confidentiality* session at the national SBC conference in Denver in October 1986, Asta Kenney, an associate with the Alan Guttmacher Institute, approvingly explained how clinic personnel assume the right to decide which medical treatment or counseling is most appropriate for a child (Kenney 1986b). In the case of abortion counseling and referral services, the staff keeps parents in the dark because, Kenney asserted, "[i]t is clearly in the child's best interests to be able to get those services." "The bottom line," she stated at the workshop, "is that you can go ahead and provide the services without parental consent, without parental notification, when you can see that the kid is going to go without services otherwise."

In the same vein, the keynote speaker at the Denver conference in 1986, Dr. James P. Comer from the Yale University Child Study Center, expressed the sentiments of many when he observed that "[t]he task of helping children to grow today to meet the needs of a complex society are just much bigger than any individual family can manage" (Comer 1986). He proposed establishing mechanisms "for changing the school to allow adults in the school to serve as *parental surrogates* to help children grow and develop" (emphasis added).

In the same opening session, Joy Dryfoos, chairman of the board of the Center for Population Options, placed the campaign to establish SBCs squarely in the middle of "the battle over the morals of the children and the never-ending game over the children's entitlement to get the capacities they need to grow into responsible adults" (Dryfoos 1986c). She also explained that she believed the clinics "are succeeding because they are helping the schools assume the role of surrogate parents—the role that society has dumped on the schools."

One important ramification of this transfer of parental authority to professionals outside of the family, according to Dryfoos, was to ensure they could do "what has to be done to ensure that the children can grow up" (Dryfoos 1986c). This battle over morals mentioned by Dryfoos is especially evident in the determination of SBCs to provide teens with abortions without parental knowledge or consent.

Many parents would be surprised to be told that health professionals in their local schools have decided that they are not doing a proper job of parenting. Such ideas would seldom, if ever, be discussed publicly as a rationale for opening clinics because it would infuriate parents and many other members of the community.

This becomes clear if we look at the results of a major national opinion poll sponsored by the Planned Parenthood Federation of America in August and September 1985. The Harris poll clearly demonstrated that parents favor retaining a strong role in making medical decisions concerning their children. Fifty-two percent of the respondents who had children ages six to eighteen favored "a federal law prohibiting family planning clinics from giving birth control assistance [which always includes abortion counseling and referrals] to teenagers unless they have received permission from their parents." Forty-four percent of parents opposed the law, and four percent were "not sure." Moreover, fifty-four percent of Blacks and fifty-six percent of Hispanics favored the law (Harris 1985, 27).

This finding that parents are not about to abandon their responsibilities and rights is especially gratifying in view of the fact that the poll was commissioned by one of leading SBC advocates and the nation's largest promoter and provider of abortions.

Contesting Pro-Life Educational Programs

Direct accessibility to teens through SBCs will help the pro-abortion forces achieve a second key objective: countering the mounting groundswell of right-to-life support among the youth. Located *inside* the school and allowed to teach health classes, the school-clinic staff has an extraordinary opening to influence what students think about abortion and how they act on those opinions. Apprehension that right-to-life advocates may be able to turn the upcoming generation of voters against abortion is one of the deep-seated fears of pro-abortion advocates (St. Martin 1986, 8; Franz 1986, 10).

In a letter sent out in August 1986 asking for help in gathering information about pro-life activities among teens, Frances Kissling, president of Catholics for a Free Choice, stressed that the Center for Population Options was "concerned about this anti-choice trend in our teenagers" (Kissling and Senderowitz 1986). The results of the survey, reported Kissling, would be available to the "pro-choice community for its internal information and may serve as a tool for future programming."

Debra Haffner, the public policy director for the Center for Population Options, reiterated these concerns during a workshop at annual meeting of the American Psychological Association in Washington, D.C. in August 1986. According to an analysis by Dr. Wanda Franz, a developmental psychologist who attended the session, Haffner believes that pro-lifers had been working much harder to educate teens than pro-abortion organizations (Franz 1986, 10). In order to better understand why teens were turning pro-life, the Center for Population Options used "focus groups" to study of teens' opinions on abortion, reported Haffner. Apparently she was not encouraged by the results, and she expressed concern over several types of right-to-life educational programs that she considered particularly effective.

Using SBCs to Guarantee Financial Survival

In addition to offering fresh ways to achieve long-standing ideological goals, school-based clinics give Planned Parenthood and its allies two possible new avenues to enhance their financial security. Since the 1960s, they maintained the same relatively narrow scope of "reproductive health services." Income grew when either legislators increased the appropriations for existing programs, such as Title X, or Planned Parenthood and its ilk were able to tap into different government programs dealing with the same areas that they had used before.

Increasing funding for current programs—even one such as Title X which has highly placed and influential Congressional backers—is never a certainty because of political pressure in the nation's capital to cut the deficit and the controversy over the abortion counseling and referrals done in those clinics. While the national family planning industry can rely on its strong supporters in Congress to promote better funding, prudence dictates that the Planned Parenthood Federation and its allies also turn to locating alternative sources of government money. Moreover, coupled with continuing uncertainties in the health-care industry, these realities have made the SBC supporters recognize that they should diversify their services beyond reproductive health in order to be able to survive financially. The school-clinic program offers the opportunity to achieve both objectives.

New Sources of Income

Since the beginning of the "Reagan Revolution" in 1981, Planned Parenthood and its allies contend that they have been under severe political pressure to prevent cuts in their funding. Between 1980 and 1985, they claim that the annual government spending for their programs, measured in constant dollars, declined 12% from approximately $342 million to approximately $300 million (Wunsch and Aved 1987, 71).

In view of the possibility of stable, or even possibly declining, levels of funding (in terms of dollars of constant value), legislative initiatives to open SBCs might be a winning strategy. Millions of dollars from all levels of government could pour into their coffers. Planned Parenthood Federation affiliates and many of the other non-profit agencies allied with them politically and philosophically could possibly qualify for the funds by adding school-based facilities.

They would certainly be prime candidates for funding under a proposed law introduced by three leading pro-abortion supporters in both the U.S. House and Senate in August 1986. (Those bills died at the end of the 99th

Congress and were reintroduced for the new Congress in March 1987) (U.S. Congress. House 1987a and 1987b; Senate 1987).

One proposal would provide $50 million per year over a four-year period to establish "school-based adolescent health services demonstration projects." Such clinics must offer abortion counseling and referrals and "maintain the confidentiality of patient records" (that is, serve teens without parental knowledge or consent) (U.S. Congress. House 1987a).

"We're optimistic about this new bill," explained Sharon Lovick, director of the Support Center for SBCs, at a workshop on March 13, 1987 at the Children's Defense Fund's annual meeting on adolescent pregnancy prevention (Lovick 1987a). She urged the attendees to join the Support Center in building support for the bills by lobbying, writing letters, and other promotional activities.

Since the initial bill specifically aimed at funding SBCs went nowhere in 1986, Congressional proponents have tried secreting SBC funding provisions in other measures that have a greater likelihood of passing, such as a school dropout prevention bill (U.S. Congress House 1987b; Senate 1987).

New State Initiatives

Battles for funding will also be going on at the state level. Jackie Schwietz, co-executive director and lobbyist for Minnesota Citizens Concerned for Life, explained at a workshop discussing state efforts to fight SBCs at the National Right to Life Convention in June 1987 that when federal money dried up, the clinic advocates in her state went to the legislature for funds to expand their operations.

In February 1986 a leading pro-abortion Minnesota state senator attempted unsuccessfully to pass a measure that would permit school districts to make arrangements with a non-profit organization to operate the SBC using federal funds funnelled through state agencies, she noted. However, when the bill was amended in committee to prohibit the funds from going to non-profits that provided abortions, the senator withdrew the bill. That key provision would have prevented Planned Parenthood and the St. Paul-Ramsey Medical Center from receiving any funds because both perform abortions (Schwietz 1987). Apparently, the clinic proponents gave higher priority to abortion advocacy than receiving funds to provide non-abortion-related medical care to teenagers.

In 1987, school-clinic advocates took an new approach by burying SBC funding in a number of bills, just as SBC proponents have done in Congress recently. "They were very creative," Schwietz explained, "and it was extremely difficult to keep track of where it was" among the more than 2,000 bills introduced (Schwietz 1987). "We were extremely fortunate that we had some legislators who picked up on some of the dangerous language," Schwietz continued, which was included in a wide variety of bills, including family life education, a recodification of the state's public health act, and an education department bill. Lobbying on the last bill necessitated a major shift from the past for MCCL, which had not lobbied regularly on education bills.

Through strong efforts and the presence of a pro-life governor and state legislature, Minnesota Citizens Concerned for Life not only prevented the SBC funding but also added important pro-life wording to the public health act. However, other states may not be in as advantageous position to turn back the momentum in the last minute in the same way. Vigilance is the watchword.

Oregon and Michigan have already approved substantial state-level appropriations for establishing and maintaining SBCs, and many more such initiatives are expected (Center for Pop. Options 1986d, 10 and 12). As explained in more detail in Chapter Eight, these state-level initiatives circumvent local opposition to clinics.

Diversification of Medical Services

In addition to offering Planned Parenthood and its allies new avenues to garner more public funds for the services that they are currently performing, operating school-based clinics would provide them with opportunities to foster long-term economic and political viability.

SBCs could increase these leading pro-abortion organizations' government support by making it possible to offer a broader range of services, such as routine physical examinations, treatment of minor illnesses, immunizations, prenatal care, nutrition education, and treatment for alcohol and drug abuse. By increasing both the sources and amounts of income, this arrangement could significantly enhance an agency's long-term stability.

Moreover, operating "comprehensive-health" clinics would provide them with a valuable opportunity to remain competitive in the health-care market by broadening their medical and administrative expertise (O'Brien 1987). Since Planned Parenthood affiliates and the other abortion providers are often affected by what goes on in other sectors of the health-care system, they monitor very closely what is happening in the industry. At present, that system is in a state of tremendous flux for a variety of reasons: changing government payment policies, rising medical malpractice costs—particularly in reproductive health, and the growth of private hospitals and health-maintenance organizations (HMOs)—to name just a few. Moreover, they face possible encroachment by HMO's or other types of service providers on their traditional monopoly of reproductive health services for indigent women and teens. The authors of an article in the March/April 1987 issue of Planned Parenthood's *Family Planning Perspectives* observed that "family planning agencies in the private sector are only just beginning to appreciate the radical changes that must be made in their administrative orientation if they are to survive intact" (Wunsch and Aved 1987, 14).

Faced with these uncertainties and the prospect of stable—perhaps even declining—government funding in the near future, Planned Parenthood and its allies could welcome the opportunity to operate SBCs. The experience gained there might help them learn how to extend their clinics' scope of activities beyond "reproductive services" into a broader range of preventive health care.

Conclusion

In summary, just as in the 1960s and early 1970s when the abortion "reform" campaign was reaching its climax, the public and policymakers have been made party to only a fraction of the vast social and political changes that proponents are anxious to achieve through school-based clinics. The in-school location enables Planned Parenthood and its allies to have the best of both worlds. They retain a quasi-official status as a private agency, but operate at the public's expense and with minimal oversight. As a autonomous agent operating the SBC, the staff adopts the practices and policies of the community-based clinic *and* gains the invaluable proximity to students and authority and legitimation of the school. (Chapter Six gives more details about the techniques used to keep parents in the dark.)

Operating SBCs offer Planned Parenthood and its allies such an outstanding opportunity to attain far-reaching ideological goals and reap substantial material benefits that they have committed substantial resources to building a groundswell of media and community support for establishing clinics throughout the country. The next chapter examines the fallacies and holes in one of their principal justifications for SBCs.

CHAPTER FIVE

MISLEADING CLAIMS ABOUT REDUCING PREGNANCIES

Introduction

When SBC proponents state their justifications for operating school-based clinics, at the heart of their case is the claim that the clinics can reduce the incidence of teen pregnancy, which should, they say, also lower the number of abortions. In fact, supporters greatly misrepresent their alleged achievements. The data about pregnancy rates from the pilot clinic programs in inner-city schools in several cities, such as St.Paul, Baltimore, and Chicago, simply is inadequate to support their overblown claims of success. Indeed, the statistics in some cases may indicate that SBCs may actually increase, rather than reduce, the number of abortions.

The opening section of this chapter briefly describes the two types of evidence offered by SBC proponents to support their claims of success. The second part examines the reasons why clinic advocates do not have the evidence to back up their claims. And the third section shows how they have attempted to hide these serious inadequacies from the public and policymakers.

SBC's Claims of "Success"

SBC advocates have presented two general types of evidence allegedly demonstrating their clinics' salutory effects in reducing teen pregnancies. One type makes a direct and emphatic connection between SBCs and the key teen behavior—pregnancy.

A few examples will illustrate how strong claims about how SBCs cut rates of teen pregnancy are standard fare among school-clinic advocates.

● In a press release sent out in September 1985 from the Ounce of Prevention Fund (a non-profit organization operating the DuSable High School clinic in Chicago), spokesman Judy Carter asserted that "[s]chool based clinics are the only pregnancy prevention programs that have demonstrated a significant reduction in the teenage pregnancy rate" (Carter 1985).

• The superintendent of schools and supervisor of health services for the St. Paul, Minnesota schools, where the four pioneer SBCs are located, wrote an article for the September 1986 edition of the periodical *The School Administrator* with the emphatic title: "School Clinics Help Curb Teen Pregnancy and Dropout Rate" (Bennett and Miller 1986, 12).

• In May 1986 Faye Wattleton, president of the Planned Parenthood Federation, praised "the often dramatic drop in teen pregnancy and childbirth rates" in schools with clinics in a Scripps-Howard news service story carried coast-to-coast (Wattleton 1986).

• The Human Resources Administration of the City of New York, an important agency strongly backing SBCs, published a fact sheet in June 1986 which declared that "[e]vidence indicates that these clinics have reduced teenage pregnancy rates and the negative consequences of teenage childbearing" (New York City 1986, 1).

• A Guttmacher Institute press release on July 9, 1986 announcing publication of Laurie Zabin's article about the Baltimore school-linked clinics asserted that "[i]nner-city high school girls participating in an experimental school-based pregnancy prevention program showed a dramatic decrease in pregnancies" (Alan Guttmacher Institute 1986, 4).

In addition to claims that SBCs reduce teen pregnancy, another type of "proof" that SBCs indirectly influence teen pregnancy rates includes showing reductions in birth rates among students, increases in usage rates of the facilities, and high approval ratings by students and the community. Two examples illustrate what SBC proponents say.

• The Center for Population Options' promotional booklet titled "School-Based Clinics: Update 1986" stated that the clinics "have demonstrated their success in a number of ways," specifically the "rapid growth in the number of programs," "students use these programs," and "[c]linics in St. Paul have demonstrated that they are effective in reducing unintended births and their effects"(Lovick and Wesson 1986, 12).

• A friendly report about the operation of the West Dallas High School clinic by reporter Marc Fisher published in the *Washington Post* on April 14, 1987 explained how the facility was "thriving" with high registration (Fisher 1987, A8). Moreover, "from 1971 to 1984," stated Fisher, "the carried pregnancy rate [usually known as the birth, or fertility, rate] declined by half among 13- and 14-year-olds, by a third among 15- and 16-year-olds and by a quarter among 17- and 18-year-olds."

Now that we have looked at the public statements from proponents about how "successful" SBCs are, let us examine the reality behind these claims.

Claims Unproven Because of Deficiencies In Pregnancy, Abortion Data

When school clinics initially became a hot news item in 1985, SBC advocates were hard pressed for proof to back up assertions that the clinics could prevent or reduce pregnancies. SBC operators had, in fact, collected data only about *births*—not *pregnancies*—of students who had attended their clinics. Even those birth statistics were not very reliable.

Thus, they could not provide reliable statistics showing the clinics' influence (if any) on pregnancy and abortion because they had not conducted the proper scientific "outcome evaluation" to measure the success of their programs.

According to a published report of the panel which conducted the study of adolescent pregnancy for the National Academy of Sciences, outcome evaluation is essential to assess "the effectiveness of an intervention strategy in achieving its specified objectives" (Hayes 1987, 250-251). Continues the report, "typically, outcome evaluation involves establishing 'before' and 'after' measures of program activity and comparing them to a control group that was not exposed to the program."

In other words, this evaluation tool provides evidence about whether (and how well) a specific method achieves a given goal. In the case of SBCs, the key issue is: Did the clinic reduce teen pregnancy and abortion rates?—which is what SBCs supposedly claimed to do. (See Appendix Three for a more detailed explanation and analysis of outcome evaluation.)

No Outcome Evaluation

Writing in the Spring 1986 issue of *Planned Parenthood Review*, Joy Dryfoos explained the proponents' dilemma. We quote her candid remarks at length because they underscore how flimsy the evidence is for clinic "successes" in reducing teen pregnancy.

In most SBCs, researchers encounter severe difficulties determining the number of pregnancies among clinic users, Dryfoos wrote, because many girls do not return after their first visit for treatment or consultation (Dryfoos 1986a, 6). "Even if we did know the [pregnancy] rates," she wrote, "we do not have a comparable control group, which would be necessary to show that the program resulted in a greater reduction in pregnancy among its participants than in the general population."

Because of the inherent problems in identifying all of the pregnant girls, researchers must try to calculate the number of pregnancies by working backward, as it were, from statistics on clearly documented events, such as births. However, that is difficult even when a program has attempted to conduct outcome evaluation—that is, by comparing data from an experimental and a non-experimental ("control") school clinic program. Dryfoos pointed out that "the search for the elusive birth rate is very time-consuming, costly, and hazardous, and, at best, tells only half the story." Moreover, "[n]o matter how refined the research methodology, it is close to impossible to track abortions, the other half of the pregnancy story," she wrote (Dryfoos 1986a, 7).

Addressing an audience of journalists in May, 1986, Dryfoos said that in the absence of "knowledge of whether or not young women are getting abortions, we really can't say whether or not the program is preventing pregnancy" (Dryfoos 1986b, 8). And since "abortions are usually underreported in personal interviews," she continued, "pregnancy rates are difficult to measure." In other words, since women who have had abortions routinely deny that fact in interviews, the researchers have great difficulty ascertaining how many pregnancies ended in abortion. (Although interviews and survey techniques are inadequate to evaluate SBC pregnancy rates, it does not rule out the possibility that other methods could provide valuable insights.)

In view of this expert's bleak assessment of the inherent obstacles to obtaining reliable information, it is no wonder that SBC proponents are at a loss to provide authoritative data about the effects of school-clinic programs.

SBC Advocates Aware Data Scarce

SBC advocates and staff members recognized the serious deficiencies in their statistical evidence well before their first national SBC conference held in November 1984.

In summarizing the results of that meeting held in Houston, Texas and of a national survey of SBC operations, Douglas Kirby, director of research for the Center for Population Options, conceded that "most of them have not yet conducted evaluations to determine the impact upon pregnancy" (Kirby 1985, 14). Likewise, after the second SBC conference in Chicago in November 1985, Asta Kenney, a Guttmacher Institute staff member, reported that "solid data on the health impact of these clinics is scarce" (Kenney 1986a, 45).

The reports by SBC proponents at the conferences also failed to provide any insights about the clinics' impact on abortion rates. For example, the clinics in St. Paul, which they often hold up as the model for others around the country, offered no reliable information on this key issue, they acknowledged. According to Kenney's report of the 1985 SBC conference, Ann Ricketts, administrator of the St. Paul clinics, was sure that the birth rate among students in the clinic schools had declined by 37 percent between 1976-1977 and 1984-1985 (Kenney 1986a, 45). However, "[w]hether the decline was due to a decrease in the number of pregnancies," Kenney commented, "or to an increase in reliance on abortion cannot be discerned."[1]

Abortion Apparent Cause of
Birth Rate Decline In Two Clinics

SBC advocates' assertions that they lack sufficient documentation to determine the cause of declining birth rates in schools with SBCs contrast sharply with statistics from two major school clinics which strongly suggest that the reductions in birth rates are due, in large measure, to an increase in abortions and *not* to a decline in pregnancies. Clinic proponents have been aware of these reports for some time, but neither has received widespread publicity outside of the SBC advocacy network.

The first was a two-year study of the Kansas City, Missouri clinic reported at the national SBC conference in 1985. According to Asta Kenney, the executive director, Gerald Kitzi, revealed that the number of girls "who said that they had never been pregnant remained about 10 percent in both years; although the proportion who reported that they had had a baby dropped slightly, from eight to six percent" (Kenney 1986a, 45).

Likewise, in the Planned Parenthood school-based clinic in Muskegon, Michigan, a three-year study showed that the birth rate "dropped from 13% before the center opened to 10.3% after the 3rd year." Yet "[t]here was no significant change in the pregnancy rate," stated the staff's report (Muskegon Area Planned Parenthood 1985a, 2).

While these findings from Kansas City and Muskegon may not reflect the trends in all SBCs nationwide, they understandably arouse suspicions among right-to-life supporters. The absence of reliable pregnancy and abortion data from other clinics serves to reinforce pro-lifers' concerns that SBC proponents are essentially fabricating success claims. The arrogant attitude of the proponents of the clinics is apparent in their reluctance, if not outright refusal, to answer the tough questions about the supposed effectiveness of SBCs in changing the behavior of teens, and especially in reducing pregnancy.

Limited Progress Noted at
1986 SBC Conference

With one notable exception mentioned below, speakers at the third annual national conference on school clinics held in October 1986 offered little that was new in the way of authoritative statistics. However, the SBC advocates are apparently trying to remedy the deficiency by starting a limited number of outcome evaluations.

During a session titled "Research Update," Douglas Kirby provided an interim report on the Center for Population Options' three-year evaluation of several clinics around the country. "In general," he observed with remarkable modesty, "I think we have learned that it is difficult to change behavior, and that we should have in general realistic expectations about the extent to which the clinics can do that" (Kirby 1986). In addition, Kirby noted, there remain "limitations in terms of our ability to document the effectiveness of our programs."

Speaking at the same general session in her capacity as a leading SBC researcher, Laurie Zabin told her fellow clinic supporters that "there are no easy solutions" to teen pregnancy (Zabin 1986a). "We really shouldn't believe that we have a handle on this problem," she remarked, especially since pregnancy is "a very, very difficult variable to assess and takes time."

Having said all this, however, did not deter her from asserting that the school-clinic research program in Baltimore that she had directed under the auspices of the Johns Hopkins University had caused a reduction in pregnancies and abortions.

The Baltimore Experiment

Once clinics began receiving more media attention in late 1985 and early 1986, proponents found themselves in a difficult position (Kenney 1986a, 44; Mathews 1985, A3). Critics were raising embarrassing questions about the dubious "proof" offered to show that the model clinic in St. Paul had decreased pregnancies. They also pointed out the inadequacy of using birth rates to measure SBC effectiveness, especially since the number of births may well have dropped because of a rise in abortions (U.S. Congress. House 1985, 380-381). Zabin's study claiming success for the Baltimore clinics dutifully celebrated in the July 1986 edition of *Family Planning Perspectives* gave SBC proponents a ready-made response to the growing skepticism about the data (Zabin et al. 1986). Typical were Zabin's comments to the *New York Times* in July 1986 when she said "I hope that the critics will be as relieved as I am to see that good professional counseling and services can protect those who are sexually active, can cut down the rate of conception among them and at the same time help those who are not sexually active to say 'no' " (Brozan 1986, C3).

Such alleged good results could not have been announced at a more propitious time for the SBC movement. The Baltimore study has had a major impact on the whole SBC debate, reported *Time* Magazine on November 24, 1986 (Leo 1986, 58). It is "one of the most frequently cited by activists who support sex education and school clinics." Although it can hardly be classified as a typical clinic arrangement, it has probably supplanted St. Paul as the "model" of what a school clinic can supposedly accomplish.

Immodest Claims of Success

Given the limitations of the study, the claims made about the "successes" in Baltimore are exceedingly immodest. According to the press release sent out by the Alan Guttmacher Institute, the researchers asserted that the pregnancy rate among inner-city girls at the experimental schools *dropped* 30.1%, while the pregnancy rate at the control schools *increased* 57.6% during the twenty-eight-month study (Alan Guttmacher Institute 1986, 4). Another major change in behavior reported by Zabin and her colleagues, which they emphasized repeatedly in speeches and interviews, was "an apparent postponement of first intercourse among high school students exposed to the program for three years." "The median length of delay (not shown [by statistics in the report]) is seven months," they stated (Zabin et al. 1986, 122).

Zabin's clinic project appeared to be all the more successful when viewed against the background of challenges to previous SBC statistics which emphasized not pregnancy rates, but birth rates. The Baltimore project allegedly measured the proper outcome—reduction of pregnancy rates.

Distinctions from Previous Clinic Programs

It is essential to draw an important distinction between the Baltimore clinics and earlier programs conducted in cities such as St. Paul, Dallas, Houston, and Kansas City. In the cities other than Baltimore, the clinic operators primarily sought to provide medical services. There were no pretensions that they had precisely measured pregnancy rates and other conditions before and after a predetermined period of time, which would have brought a reliable "outcome evaluation." They simply are not set up to collect that type of information.

By contrast, the Baltimore program, funded from 1981 through 1984 by several pro-abortion foundations, operated as a demonstration project (Zabin et al. 1984; 1986, 19). The objective of the experiment was to compare the changes in pregnancy rates, contraceptive patterns, sexual knowledge, and other factors among the students. The team collected information from the students through a series of surveys using anonymous questionnaires.

In the study, one junior high school and one senior high school (the "program" schools) each had a medical facility located adjacent to them, either across the street or a few blocks away (Zabin et al. 1984, 425). The clinic staff operated an outreach office within each school to arrange appointments in the clinic, mingled with the students in the halls, and taught health education classes. This arrangement is defined as a "school-linked," rather than "school-based," clinic.

The other study group consisted of another pair of junior and senior high schools without clinics (the "control" schools). The student bodies in both sets of schools were supposed to be similar. However, as it turned out, they were anything but.

Exaggerations and Methodological Flaws

Press accounts of the Baltimore study have unfortunately fallen into the pattern established by accounts written about the St. Paul program of uncritically accepting assertions made by SBC advocates. In this case, however, the error is somewhat more understandable in view of the study's greater methodological complexity.

Questions Arise Over
Four External Factors

Those unwilling to mindlessly accept the claims of success are more alert to the study's flaws. First, critics point to four external factors that may have dramatically influenced the outcome of the study.

• Neither the article in *Family Planning Perspectives* nor press accounts have mentioned the inherent conflict of interest of Laurie Zabin, the principal researcher on the project, who currently serves as the chairman of the board of the Alan Guttmacher Institute and member of the national board of the Planned Parenthood Federation of America (Planned Parenthood 1987a, 30; Alan Guttmacher Institute 1985, 23).

• The research team failed to evaluate how the social and cultural milieu of the community surrounding the schools effected the outcome of the experimental program.

• The Johns Hopkins group failed to explain why research conducted on four urban schools, chosen solely because of their proximity to Johns Hopkins University (Zabin 1986b, 10), should have any general applicability to the tens of thousands of other junior and senior high schools across the nation. In fact, according to the NRC report *Risking The Future* (which vigorously supported establishment of SBCs), the Baltimore "clinic model differs some-what from the typical school-based clinic" (Hayes 1987, 173). With the primary health facilities off campus, the Baltimore clinics are classified as school-*linked*, rather than school-*based*. Both Zabin and the NRC panel acknowledged that the school-linked clinics may not be appropriate for most circumstances (Zabin et al. 1986; Hayes 1987, 173).

• The research team did not explain why policymakers should base major policy decisions involving hundreds of thousands of dollars on information from a solitary research project, especially in view of its methodological deficiencies. Stan Weed, director of the Institute for Research and Evaluation in Salt Lake City, writing in the October 14, 1986 issue of *The Wall Street Journal* pointed out that a "single study of any one particular program has inherent limitations, both as a scientific statement and as a reliable guide for policy decisions" (Weed 1986, 22).

Five Flaws in Project
Design and Interpretation

In addition to the external factors, analysts have pointed out five serious shortcomings in the methodology used in the study itself. A complete descrip-tion of these flaws would be quite lengthy and not meet our immediate needs. Therefore, we will focus on the criticisms of some of the most serious defi-ciencies in the design of the study made by experts such as Jo Ann Gasper, a leading national authority on teen pregnancy.

In testimony given before a Virginia legislative committee September 5, 1986, Mrs. Gasper, who was then serving as the Deputy Assistant Secretary for Population Affairs in the U.S. Department of Health and Human Services, urged "caution in interpreting the very positive results" showing declines in pregnancy rates (Gasper 1986). Gasper stressed, for example, that the pub-lished study failed to provide data and information about the methodology that would be essential for an objective critique. In other words, without specific details about the research methods, independent experts could not determine if the study and the conclusions were valid.

Tobin Demsko, a sociologist and research analyst with the Family Research Council in Washington, D.C., provided the most comprehensive list of the Baltimore study's deficiencies in a fine research paper released by the Council in March 1987. Five points are of interest here.

• According to Demsko, Zabin and her team failed to "control [adjust] for student mobility (transfers, drop-outs, etc.) in and out of the control and experimental schools" (Demsko 1987, 8). Professor Jacqueline R. Kasun, an expert in teen pregnancy research, has noted that the researchers failed to explain why the dropout rate among the girls in the experimental (clinic) school was three times the dropout rate of girls in the control (non-clinic) schools (Kasun 1986). This issue is vitally important, stressed Kasun, because "as many as one-half of such drop-outs may be due to pregnancy." Therefore, she stated, "the omission of these girls represents a major loss of information and casts serious doubt on the study's conclusion that the clinic program reduced sex activity and pregnancy."

• Demsko shared the Kasun's misgivings that the "author's failure to give numbers, rather than percentages or percent changes, in any of the categories studied, conceals the fact that the numbers are very small in many cases" (Demsko 1987, 10). Therefore, a shift in answers from a mere handful of girls would radically influence the outcome of the study.

• Demsko noted that the team from Johns Hopkins failed to account for a "testing effect" that have resulted from administering the survey questionnaires twice at the control school but four times at the experimental school (Demsko 1987, 10). Social scientists know that the subjects of a study (in this case, the students) may act differently when they realize that they are part of a test.

Moreover, the method for collecting the information from the students may be suspect because the Baltimore project relied exclusively on self-administered surveys to collect information about the students' sexual activity, before and after the clinic program. During the "Research Update" general session at the 1986 annual national SBC conference, Gerald Kitzi, executive director of one of the nation's leading clinic programs located in Kansas City, followed Zabin to the podium just after she made her claims about the "success" of her project (Kitzi 1986).

While presenting survey data about his own programs, Kitzi questioned the reliability of the technique. Although statisticians had verified the results of a survey of sexual activity, he recognized that the results did not fit with his personal experience. In his opinion, the number of boys who had experienced intercourse could not possibly have been as high as the survey showed (Kitzi 1986).

• The researchers in Baltimore failed to list the demographic characteristics of the students who were surveyed, such as marital status, academic achievement, and family traits; therefore, analysts cannot make an independent assessment of the relative influence that these important factors had on pregnancy rates (Demsko 1987, 11).

• According to Demsko, two other considerations may have influenced the outcome of the study, but the researchers failed to account for them in their published report. Assessing the degree of influence of both the presence of a "magnet" program for gifted students in the one school—and not the other, and the differing pregnancy rates between the sets of schools prior to the beginning of the experiment is impossible without additional information (Demsko 1987, 2).

In conclusion, the status of the Baltimore study was summarized quite well by Anne Gribben, a member of the minority staff of the U.S. House of Representatives Select Committee on Children, Youth, and Families, during her testimony on September 5, 1986 at a Virginia legislative hearing. "Because reports of this study," she observed, "fail to include some very pertinent information, they leave us with as many questions as when we started" (Gribben 1986).

Statistics on Pregnancy Questionable

SBC advocates reluctantly acknowledge among themselves that they have not collected reliable statistics demonstrating that school clinics reduce teen pregnancy rates. As we have seen, experts such as Joy Dryfoos realize that SBCs should have conducted controlled studies (outcome evaluations) to supply that essential data, but they also recognize that significant practical and methodological obstacles have prevented that from occurring.

When we analyze the claims of effectiveness made for the St. Paul and Baltimore clinics, the best we can say is that they remain unproven. At worst, evidence from the school-based clinics in Michigan and Missouri points to the inevitable conclusion that the teen birthrate dropped because the girls procured more abortions, not because their pregnancy rates went down.

Diverting Attention, Disguising Intentions

Typically, in view of the deficiencies of pregnancy and abortion data, clinic proponents often successfully dodge revealing that they cannot prove that SBCs reduce teen pregnancies, by suggesting other far less meaningful measures of "success."

Replacing Pregnancy Rates With Birth Rates

One of the methods most widely used by SBC advocates to shift attention is to blur the distinction between reducing teen *pregnancy rates* and reducing teen *birth rates*. Many legislators and policymakers were fooled by this ploy of replacing the sought-after outcome (reducing teen pregnancies) with a misleading one (reducing teen births).

Since the researchers are comparing conditions "before" and "after" the clinic has been in operation, they appear to be using the more reliable "outcome" evaluation method to check whether the clinic is meeting its goals. In a grotesque sense, this may be true, but probably at the expense of the lives of unborn babies. A reduction in the birth rate may well mean that the teens were having more abortions!

The nationwide movement to establish school-based clinics took off, in no small measure, thanks to the unrebutted claims made about the "successful" program in St. Paul, Minnesota operated from 1973 through 1986 under the auspices of the St. Paul-Ramsey Medical Center. Proponents used it as the principal example of what such a program could achieve. Ironically, SBC proponents themselves have provided documentation that clinics in St. Paul, Minnesota and other cities were "successful" only because they reduced births.

For example, in a Scripps-Howard news service story carried coast-to-coast in May 1986, Faye Wattleton, Planned Parenthood's president, praised the St. Paul SBC. In that school-clinic, she asserted, "teen birth rates declined from 59 per 1,000 students in 1977 to 37 per 1,000 in 1985" (Wattleton 1986). To an uninitiated observer, these results seem quite impressive.

But it was not just Planned Parenthood making these claims. A story appearing in the *Washington Post* on December 7, 1985 illustrates the influence exerted by reports of the St. Paul programs's alleged "successes." Los Angeles approved a "pilot clinic," stated the story, based on information that "high school pregnancy rates dropped 64 percent in the first three years of a similar program in St. Paul, Minn." (Mathews 1985, A3).

These glowing reports about the St. Paul clinic epitomize the "bait and switch" technique. Proponents grab the headlines with announcements that the program reduces pregnancy rates when in fact their statistical evidence shows a reduction in births (sometimes also described as "fertility," or even "carried pregnancy"), not pregnancies.

Reporters, in turn, either out of error or for other motives, continue to blur the distinction. The cover story in the December 9, 1985 issue of *Time* magazine is a perfect example. Titled "Children Having Children," the article reported the claim by clinic proponent Douglas Kirby that the "pregnancy rate drops sharply" after the clinics start (Wallis 1985, 89). But when the author of the *Time* article, Claudia Wallis, went on to describe the "model" project in St. Paul, she wrote that it had brought a "dramatic" decline in the *birth rate* among the students.

Wallis's confusion about pregnancies and births in her *Time* article is, unfortunately, quite typical; and the press and many policymakers have been accepting the claims uncritically.

Juggling the Evaluation Methods

Faced with the necessity to justify their programs, clinic staffs and proponents often avoid the whole issue of evaluating the outcome of clinic programs by substituting an evaluation based on client attendance rates or acceptance by the students. Both of these measures, classified by professional researchers as "process evaluation," are only marginally related to the clinic's "bottom line" of reducing teen pregnancies. (See Appendix Three for a more detailed explanation and analysis of "process evaluation.")

Because the results of process evaluation are presented in statistical form, many people might not recognize how they are being misled. Numbers on paper somehow gives the information credibility, especially when it is offered and interpreted by an apparently authoritative source. However, in this case, the facts derived through "process evaluation" does not tell us what we want—and need—to know.

Joy Dryfoos explained why using process evaluation is so important to SBC proponents. In the spring 1986 issue of *Planned Parenthood Review*, she suggested that "because pregnancy outcomes are so difficult to track and to relate to programs, it would be easier for all of us [in the family planning industry, presumably] if decision makers would be satisfied with contraceptive use as a surrogate [a substitute] for pregnancy prevention" (Dryfoos 1986a, 17).

Dryfoos' comment is most revealing. She cannot prove that SBCs are accomplishing their goal—pregnancy prevention; therefore, Dryfoos asks decisionmakers to accept as a substitute what she can prove—they are distributing their services well. Note that Dryfoos has replaced means (distribution) for ends (pregnancy prevention).

Douglas Kirby shared Dryfoos's enthusiasm for substituting other criteria. His suggestions included measuring attendance rates at the clinic, the ability to prevent school dropouts by pregnant girls, the level of community acceptance, or changes in the general health of inner-city youths (Kirby 1985, 13-14).

Conclusion

Because reporters do not mention the ambiguities associated with the claims that school clinics reduce teen pregnancies, the media's willingness to accept claims of success has played a major role in increasing support among the general public and local officials. As we have seen, while the claims are totally without foundation, the SBC proponents have cleverly avoided coming to grips with the deficiencies in their own statistics.

A brief mention of one last method that SBC advocates are using to get funding might be valuable. SBC proponents may attempt to stress how the services aimed at reducing teen pregnancy are but a small part of the comprehensive program offered by the clinic. They accuse critics of focusing exclusively on the controversial aspects while failing to see the bigger picture of benefits to the students as a whole.

One answer to this accusation is to point out how the "comprehensive" services are actually an smokescreen for the real agenda, as pointed out above in Chapter Two. Another response is to stress that all facets of a program should be evaluated separately. As we have seen, the clinics have not reduced teen pregnancies, and decisionmakers should not fund any portion of a school clinic program without authoritative proof that it is effective in achieving the goals.

Decisionmakers should not be misled into accepting inaccurate and unsupported claims. In addition to promoting abortion, clinics are not effective in achieving their key objective of reducing teen pregnancies. Therefore, schools should not have them and the public should not be funding them.

CHAPTER SIX

UNDERCUTTING PARENTAL AUTHORITY

I n view of the obvious signs coming from public opinion polls and how frequently controversy surrounds school-based clinics, particularly over the issue of parental involvement, clinic advocates feel it is prudent to maintain the appearance of involving parents and obtaining their consent to "treat" their children. Yet a closer examination of how SBC policies work in practice demonstrates that the advocates frequently believe that parents must be cut out in order for advocates to operate clinics effectively.

SBC advocates customarily set out to accomplish this goal in two ways. First, while the clinic is being established, they often manipulate the governmental policy process to maximize their own influence and minimize community input in setting the clinic's policies. Second, after the SBC opens, the staff provides teens with "confidential treatment"—that is, without the parents' involvement—by either ignoring or circumventing parental consent procedures.

Setting Policies
Without Parental Involvement

We can gain insight into how SBC proponents manipulate the policy-making process in many communities to exclude parents and community leaders by examining speeches and literature from SBC proponents and examining reports which detail how clinics were established around the country.

The desire of parents and the public at large received minor attention in Douglas Kirby's authoritative study of SBCs (Kirby 1985). In fact, he mentions parents only three times in his extensive four-page, nineteen-step explanation of the "Program Implementation" process. It is abundantly clear that SBC promoters will not let the parents have any meaningful input into the process unless they will lend support to the clinic. For example, when the important work begins with the selection of members for an advisory committee, Kirby recommends that the representatives "[i]nclude only people who are basically supportive of the idea" (Kirby 1985, 19). The members of this carefully selected group work behind the scenes and "try to maintain a low profile," in Kirby's words (Kirby 1985, 21).

The pattern of activity by clinic advocates in Cincinnati, Pittsburgh, and Portland, Maine, for example, closely paralleled what Kirby prescribed. Parents were left out of the decision-making process unless they protested. A carefully selected group worked behind the scenes lining up support before any public announcement was made of the possibility of opening a clinic (Crockett and Theis 1986, A1; Doss 1986, A1; Coughlan 1987a).

Pro Forma Parental Consent

Aware that parents want to be involved in decisions about their children, most clinics require nominal parental consent. However, they have employed some highly questionable methods to trivialize parental involvement.

SBCs often distribute parental consent forms that are so vague as to provide the clinics with virtual carte blanche. Joy Dryfoos listed several examples, including having parents "sign a blanket consent form unrelated to any specific clinic visit," or have the consent form "apply for the entire period of the student's enrollment" (Dryfoos 1985b, 73).

Even more disingenuous is the approach of the SBC operated by Planned Parenthood of Muskegon, Michigan which utilizes a "negative" checkoff system. The clinic staff mails home a form and chooses to *assume* that the parent has authorized treatment *unless* the parent signs and returns the form to prevent it. Only one percent of the forms were returned to the school (Muskegon Area Planned Parenthood 1986b, 1).

Moreover, as we saw in Chapter Two, SBCs circumvent restrictions on their activities by referring teenagers to outside agencies which will provide the prohibited services. In cases where either the parental form or school policy prevents a certain kind of "treatment" such as abortion counseling, the staff can arrange for it through a referral.[1]

Control and Funding By Outside Agencies

Another, more subtle approach used by SBCs to circumvent parental consent is arranging for an outside organization or agency other than the school district to operate the clinics. Or, if that is not possible, they arrange for the clinic to receive funding from a government source, which obliges the clinic to follow the state's or federal agency's regulations. (This does not absolve the school district from legal liability, however, as we shall discuss in the next chapter.)

These links between schools and the outside organization have two ramifications seriously detrimental to parents' rights. First, the leaders of the private agency are not elected—therefore, not answerable directly to the public for their actions. As we have seen in earlier chapters, this insulation from parental and community influence is no accident.

Second, when an organization other than the school district operates the clinic, observed Joy Dryfoos, the facility's "medical practice is not covered by school law" (Dryfoos 1985b, 72). According to Terrance Kernan, a senior official with the strongly pro-SBC Robert Wood Johnson Foundation, this arrangement allows the medical care to be governed by the "norms of professional jurisdiction and control" (Keenan 1985, 6), which is to say the standard Planned-Parenthood policy of keeping the parents in the dark.

The problem of autonomous private agencies keeping parents in the dark is particularly important since most clinics are operated in this way. According to the Center for Population Options' survey conducted in 1986, the majority of SBCs "are extensions of hospitals and public health departments; they are not run by the school system" (Lovick and Wesson 1986, 4). In fact, the survey found only one school system operating a clinic out of the 30 institutional sponsors. The survey separated the sponsorship of the 61 clinics then in operation into six categories: 33% by hospital/medical centers; 23% by departments of public health; 20% by non-profit organizations; 17% by community health clinics; 4% by school systems; and 3% by family planning agencies.[2]

Two examples illustrate the adverse impact of these policies in practice. First, in San Francisco, the Balboa High School clinic adopted the policy of its sponsoring agency, the city's Department of Public Health, of keeping teenagers' records confidential. According to Steve Purser, founder and administrator of the clinic, "[t]he parents don't have access to the health care file" (Purser 1986). Second, in Chicago, a private and non-profit corporation, the Ounce of Prevention Fund, operates the DuSable and Orr clinics and does confidential abortion referrals. After a controversy erupted in September 1985 just after the opening of the DuSable clinic, the *Chicago Sun-Times* reported an interview with the president of the board of education, George Munoz, who "said that because the clinic is privately financed by a group of foundations, 'I'm not sure we can prohibit what medical assistance they can provide' " (O'Connor 1985, 6).

SBCs also use their receipt of certain types of funding as justification to cut parents out of the key decisions. For example, as we have seen in chapter two, if the agency operating the clinic receives federal Title X funding, federal rules requiring confidential abortion counseling and referrals supersede and nullify any local or state requirements for parental consent or notification prior to medical treatment. Moreover, the same type of restrictions apply if state funds used in clinics carry any strings because, as Jodie Levin-Epstein, the Center for Population Options's director of public policy, pointed out at a conference in 1986, the "state is going to be in the business of trying to determine regulations and guidelines" (Levin-Epstein 1986a).[3]

Hiding Records From Parents

The clinic staff's compulsion for keeping parents unaware of what is happening to their children is so strong that they have resorted to literally keeping two sets of books. This kind of blatant duplicity makes "sense" when we understand that SBC proponents are determined to act as "parents."

Clinic staff members in the audience at the "Parents: Consent and Confidentiality" session of the SBC national conference in October 1986 described several ways to maintain confidentiality (Center for Pop. Options 1986e). One ploy is for the nurse to keep records about confidential services in her desk as part of "her own papers," which are to be considered her personal property. Another apparently common tactic is to maintain two sets of health records for each student. One file has general health information to show to the parents, and another file contains confidential data which would not be shown to tham. A school nurse from New Mexico in the audience explained the procedure: "We keep separate page for each type of service provided to a student," she stated. "The ones related to family planning or other services the kids don't want their parents to know about are flagged. Then, if they [the parents] ask to see the file, we just remove the flagged pages."

Conclusion

Pro-life supporters are particularly sensitive to the issues of parental rights since abortionists routinely perform abortions on minor girls without parental knowledge or consent. SBCs undermine the parents' authority and responsibility by administering pregnancy tests, performing counseling, and referring their minor daughters for abortions without parental knowledge or consent.

One can easily foresee that with a captive clientele of "sexually active" students, the school clinic will funnel young pregnant girls off to obtain abortions under the cloak of "confidentiality." Parents must ensure that any proposals for medical treatment include adequate provision to ensure a strong parental role.

CHAPTER SEVEN

OTHER CRITICISMS OF SBCS EMERGE

U p to now we have primarily criticized SBCs for performing or promoting abortion counseling and referrals. We have also pointed out how they undermine parental rights and have proven ineffective in reducing teen pregnancies. In addition to these three issues, citizens groups around the country have raised other economic, social, and moral objections which have played a key role in either delaying and even stopping the establishment and funding of SBCs. Five key problems stand out:

- low cost-effectiveness and high overhead expenses,
- the necessity for eventual government funding,
- the possible exposure of schools to expensive medical liability lawsuits,
- forcing the overburdened educational system to handle health-care problems, and
- practicing a subtle form of racism by targeting inner-city minority teenagers as the "beneficiaries" of SBCs.

High Expense and Low Cost-Effectiveness

In view of the intense public concern about rising taxes and government spending, it is no surprise that the high cost of operating school clinics would also receive increasing attention. Criticisms of SBCs on economic grounds are twofold. School-based clinics are very expensive whether analyzed in terms of the average cost per student, the cost per visit, or the overall annual budget.

When SBC proponents are asked for specific information about the total cost of running a SBC, they offer a wide range of figures. Typically the total expenses average at least $100,000 per year. A survey of clinics reported in April 1985 by Douglas Kirby revealed that costs for a single facility varied from $25,000 to $250,000 per year, depending on the number of patients and the types of services offered (Kirby 1985, 15). In an article published about the same time, Joy Dryfoos cited the former administrator of the St. Paul clinic as her authority when she used the figure $90,000 as the "amount needed to operate a full-time high school clinic once it has been equipped" (Dryfoos 1985b, 74).

Recent data from eight clinics in New York City published in November 1986 by the *New York Times* revealed that they cost a total of $694,285 to operate for one school year (September 1985 to June 1986), or an average cost of $86,785 per clinic (Hurley 1986, C1). Another example provided in the "Working Manual" from the St. Paul SBC program shows $107,335 in total operating expenses per clinic during 1986 (Ahartz 1986, 100-101).

A second possible method of analyzing the economics of SBCs is to determine the cost per patient (student) per year. This standardized measurement offers the advantage of allowing us to project the level of expenditures that may be required if clinics were opened in other schools. In 1985, Douglas Kirby estimated that the price could vary from $100 to $125 per patient per year (Kirby 1985, 13). And clinic advocates have reported that 70% to 90% of the student body use the clinic (Perkes 1987).

A specific example illustrates how we can use Kirby's figure to estimate the annual budget for a proposed clinic. In a secondary school with 1,000 students where 70% of the student body uses the clinic, the total projected annual expense would be at least $70,000 and as high as $87,500 (i.e., 1,000 [the student body] times $100 [cost per client] times .7 [70% usage rate] equals $70,000).

Keep in mind that this was a *conservative estimate* dealing with only *one school* for only *one school year*. Large cities with many sizable schools could easily be spending over a million dollars per year to maintain a series of clinics. All of this expense would, of course, be in addition to the current school educational budget.

Looking at clinic costs from the perspective of the expense per visit can also be instructive. The *New York Times* reported that the eight New York City clinics spent $694,285 for 17,598 student visits during the 1985-1986 school year (Hurley 1986, C1). This averages out to $39.45 per visit. Dr. Joseph Zanga, chairman of the school health committee of the American Academy of Pediatrics (the nation's largest association of physicians who primarily treat adolescents and children), analyzed data from the St. Paul SBCs to arrive at a cost of $36.88 per visit (Zanga 1986). As described in the following section, he stated at a speech at a national convention of health-care professionals that these charges seem overly expensive when compared to private health-care providers.

Questionable Cost Effectiveness

In addition to objecting to the high expense of SBSs, critics have pointed out that there are much more cost-effective—and less controversial—ways to deliver services to inner-city teenagers, if health care is the goal. In some cases, the SBCs may be duplicating services that are already available in the community.

Even if conceding that government officials should turn more attention to helping medically underserved teenagers, the question remains whether a school clinic is the most effective and least costly way to dispense medical care. Joy Dryfoos acknowledged in March 1985 that "cost data for school-based clinics are rough estimates, so their cost effectiveness is not proven" (Dryfoos 1985b, 75). "The assessment of local needs will not necessarily support the setting up of a SBC," observed Lynne Gustafson, head of the school nurse services in Manchester, Connecticut and president-elect of the National Association of School Nurses (NASN), in an article in her organization's magazine in April 1987 (Lordi 1987b, 26). "In some areas," she commented, "they're just not cost-effective." (NASN's other apprehensions about SBCs were described in Chapter One.)

Dr. Joseph Zanga analyzed the relationship of costs and services very effectively and authoritatively in a workshop conducted at the annual meeting of the American Public Health Association in 1986. He found two serious deficiencies in SBCs.

He pointed out that school-based clinics fail to provide continuous and comprehensive care (Zanga 1986). Where can teens turn for services outside of school hours, on weekends, and during the summer months? "A study done in Baltimore recently," Zanga stated, "indicates that much of our pediatrician's work is done after hours?" Since school clinics are closed at that time, students must use the "local hospital emergency room—an expensive, discontinuous, non-comprehensive, stop-gap measure, at best," he observed. For example, both the DuSable and Orr clinics in Chicago, for example, are only open from 8:00 A.M. until 4:00 P.M. (Ounce of Prevention Fund 1986).

A brief amplification on this point beyond what Dr. Zanga discussed might be useful. Drop-outs and high school graduates may need health care but cannot use school-based facilities. "Because of school restrictions on non-students entering the building," stated Kirby, "these clinics often cannot serve teenagers who have dropped out of school" (Kirby 1985, 11). "This is an important population of young people who could benefit from such services," he continued, "because their health needs are unusually high and they are especially likely to become pregnant."

Another deficiency of SBCs, observed Zanga, is that "when compared to private-practice options, care in school-based clinics is expensive" (Zanga 1986). For example, by comparing data on costs from the St. Paul and Chicago clinics, he found that "routine care in a pediatrician's office is about $30 per visit," but the cost in a SBC is "between $35 and $55 per visit."

The SBCs may also duplicate services that other facilities in the area are already providing to low-income teenagers. The Boston School Health Project Proposal, which recommended opening SBCs, admitted that the "majority of Boston's poor residents have access to quality health care via Medicaid, Medicare and such programs as Project Good Health and Healthy Start" (quoted in Archdiocese of Boston 1987, 16). Moreover, pointed out the report, adolescents have both "availability and geographic access to health care."

Dr. John C. Willke, president of the National Right to Life Committee, pointed out specific examples of how the teenagers' needs can largely be met by community resources. The students do not require an in-school clinic for athletic injuries or other trauma because those can only be handled at a hospital emergency room, he explained. Routine immunizations, school and work physicals, and illnesses such as fever, cough, and infections are handled through public-health clinics or private physicians. Furthermore, the public should keep in mind, Dr. Willke observed, that the preteens and teens are the healthiest years of a child's life (Willke 1987).

Certainly, issues such as these played an important part in the formulation of the American Academy of Pediatrics' "Guidelines" on SBCs published in April 1987, which stated that "questions regarding the efficacy of school-based health clinics remain unresolved." The policy committee gave what could be characterized as luke-warm support for "selective implementation of school-based health programs in areas where the health needs of the school age population are not being met" (American Academy 1987). Certainly, there would be few such circumstances.

If improving the health care to teenagers is really a top priority for policymakers, then the evidence clearly shows that there are more effective and less costly ways than school-based clinics to accomplish that goal.

Government Funding Inevitable

Another major objection raised against SBCs is the necessity for government funding once private funding runs out, usually after only a few years. An important fact, often overlooked in discussions about opening clinics, is that foundations currently supply almost a third (31%) of the current SBC funding (Lovick and Wesson 1986, 13). However, private support will not continue indefinitely.

In a refreshingly objective observation, Joy Dryfoos explained that "[a]lthough it is not fashionable to suggest that long-term viability depends on federal funding, it is difficult to imagine that foundations will be willing to support these programs permanently, except for special studies" (Dryfoos 1985b, 75). In the same article, Dryfoos also pointed out that "[a]lthough private funds have played an important part in starting up these programs, almost all of these school programs look to public support for continuation" (Dryfoos 1985b, 73).

Caught up in the enthusiasm to compete for the available foundation grants, policymakers have paid scant attention to what will happen five years (or less) down the road. Experience shows that there will be only a slim chance of closing down a SBC program—no matter how inefficient and costly—because it builds up momentum and acquires a constituency of paid staff. Therefore, policymakers need to look at the anticipated future costs before the clinics are opened. The lesson is to recognize that after the initial private start-up funds are exhausted, schools and cities will have to spend untold thousands of their own scarce tax dollars to keep the SBCs operating.

Medical Liability Open-Ended Question

In addition to recognizing that SBCs will inevitably turn to the government for operating support, policymakers should also realize that the local government or school board might be forced to pay thousands of dollars of medical expenses and lawyer's fees for students injured by the clinic's staff.

When fears are expressed about a school's or city's potential exposure to liability costs, clinic proponents offer two observations in hopes of calming worried officials. In response to a question about possible liability during a workshop at the annual meeting of the Childrens' Defense Fund in March 1987, Sharon Lovick, director of Center for Population Options' Support Center for SBCs, offered two suggestions. She urged SBC proponents to stress that the preventative health services that clinics offer are "not invasive, so they are not high risk with regard to issues of liability" (Lovick 1987a).

Another approach to minimize the risks, Lovick explained, is to "create layers of liability." The health-care providers who work part-time in the clinic maintain their own insurance coverage. The clinic pays for the insurance of their permanent staff, and the school "has its liability that extends to anything that happens in its building," she stated (Lovick 1987a).

In view of Lovick's position in the center of activities promoting SBCs, and the fact that she was appearing before a friendly audience who would probably use her suggestions to defend clinics, her observations can probably be regarded as the best answer that SBC advocates have been able to find on the liability question. However, her two observations are informative, but not convincing.

A prudent public servant will immediately realize that accidents could unfortunately happen during the least "invasive" medical services. Moreover, Lovick failed to point out the higher liability risks attached to reproductive health services, such as counseling and referrals for abortion, which after all is surgery.

In addition, even if the government is protected behind the most elaborately constructed system of layers of liability protection, it is still vulnerable. Policymakers should realize the fact that the agency operating the clinic, such as the local Planned Parenthood, carries most of the burden for liability under its insurance plan, affords limited protection to the school board (Toni Hicks 1986, 44-49). The school district or city government *will* ultimately be dragged into medical liability lawsuits because they have the "deepest pocket." Even Lovick acknowledged that "there is no way that you can, more or less, protect anybody; I mean, you can't prevent anybody from suing you" (Lovick 1987a). Moreover, the government will have to spend taxpayers' funds to defend itself, whether or not it expects to win.

In view of the medical insurance crisis and the possibility that an injured student might sue, prudence dictates that school board and city council members should think twice about sponsoring a clinic.

School Clinics Divert Vital Resources

Critics have also stressed how SBCs divert vitally needed resources away from the schools' core educational mission. In at least three cities, school board members have opposed SBCs clinics on the grounds that they represented an unnecessary diversions from the basic reason for operating schools. "We, the public school system, cannot take on and solve all society's ills. We must keep a narrower focus," said Kay Davis, a San Diego school board member who was instrumental in winning board rejection of a school-clinic program (Reynolds 1986, B1, B4).

Lou Cook, chairman of the school board in Alexandria, Virginia, echoed those views in April 1986 when a similar proposal was raised in her community. "We have no space for a clinic, no funds to support it. . . . Furthermore, there are limits to how much a school system should be held responsible for," she explained (Lou Cook, 1986).

"Why is it that the Milwaukee Public Schools are always asked to cure the ills of society?" asked Lawrence O'Neill in October 1986 after being on the losing side of a 5-to-2 vote establishing a clinic in Milwaukee, Wisconsin (Cole 1986).

U.S. Secretary of Education William Bennett, a leader in calling for a renewed stress in schools on the basic learning skills of math, English, history, and science, also has spoken out against the school clinics as a serious distraction of the schools from their basic mission (Bennett 1986; Richburg 1986).

In this connection, the coordinator of nursing services for the Albuquerque, New Mexico public schools, Ms. Greenburg, observed that "a full-time SBC may not recognize that the primary focus should be on the student's education," in an article in the April 1987 issue of *School Nurse* (Lordi 1987c, 38). She also pointed out that the SBC staff "often see a narrow clinical picture— not the school picture; and they may pull kids out of the classroom for too long."

Scott Thomson, executive director of the National Association of Secondary School Principals, agreed with these comments and added another valuable perspective of the professional educators who are being caught in the middle of a bitter fight. "We would prefer that schools not be given another job," he said. "It's a hot political issue, what's more a no-win situation for the school." "You win the support of those who want it but lose the support of those opposing," Thomson observed (*Times-West Virginian* 1986).

Clinics Send a Racist Message

School-based clinics have also come under fire from Black community leaders in many cities who denounced the racist attitudes on display in targeting SBCs almost exclusively in inner-city Black and other minority-dominated city schools. Douglas Kirby's comprehensive nationwide survey of clinics in 1985 revealed that most SBCs were located in low-income areas, and many in inner-city schools. "Most of the schools are in predominantly black areas," he explained, "but a few (e.g. Minneapolis) serve a majority of whites and a few (e.g. Dallas, San Francisco, and St. Paul) serve Hispanic, Filipino, or Southeast Asian students" (Kirby 1985, 10). A report about Black resistance to SBCs in the November 12, 1985 issue of *Education Week* stated that "although no firm statistics are available, most sources indicated that a majority of those 71 [school-based] clinics may be located in schools with large minority-group enrollments" (Viadero 1986, 13).

While proponents of clinics acknowledge that the majority of SBCs are located in inner-city areas, they believe that the arrangement is fully justified. Observed *Education Week*, advocates "stress that school clinics were designed to provide comprehensive health care to a population that, because of its age or economic status, often may not receive adequate medical attention" (Viadero 1986, 13).

Some prominent Blacks have lined up behind SBCs. For example, John E. Jacob, president of the National Urban League, and Marion Wright Edelman, president of the Children's Defense Fund (CDF) have endorsed school clinics (Jacob 1987, 6; for CDF see Chapter Three).

However, critics from a wide variety of backgrounds are not convinced. One reason may be the increasing awareness among Black leaders of the fact that pregnant Black teenagers are almost twice as likely to abort than white teenagers. For example, Kay James, president of Black Americans For Life, explained in the Congressional Black Caucus magazine that "those of us involved in the pro-life movement recognize that abortion is being offered as a primary tool in lowering the rate of teen births" (James 1987, 25).

It is also important to point out that typically organizations from outside of the Black community—not parents from the school where the clinic is located—initiate action to establish the clinic. The people most affected by the clinic did not request it for their children; but the SBC is imposed on them because someone outside of the community believes that it is worthwhile.

Chicago

On October 16, 1986, a group of thirteen Chicago Black ministers, led by the Reverend Hiram Crawford, in conjunction with two parents and two students filed a lawsuit against the SBC operating in the all-Black DuSable High School. They charged in their suit that "[t]he clinic program is a calcu- lated, pernicious effort to destroy the very fabric of family life among black parents and their children" (Associated Press 1986, A24; Crawford v. Board of Education 1986).

"If these clinics are so good for black kids, why don't they put them in white areas?" Reverend Crawford was quoted as saying in an article in the November 24, 1986 issue of *TIME.* "It's a form of genocide," he stated. "Why do they so readily recommend abortion?" (Leo 1986, 58).

Pastor Crawford has also rebutted claims by SBC proponents that parents support the clinics. He pointed out the social pressures that prevent parents from publicly challenging the school administration. Parents who are holding down two jobs and are not able to read and write well are intimidated by the clinic operators who have the authority of the city government and school board behind them, he noted.

Moreover, according to the lawsuit filed by Crawford's group, at clinics such as DuSable Clinic in south Chicago, parents face a terrible dilemma.

They must sign the consent form which gives blanket permission for the clinic to give their child all of the "services," including some they believe are immoral, and undercut their parental rights. Or, the parents can decide to not sign the consent form, which cuts their child off from any health care at the clinic (Crawford v. Board of Education). For many of the parents, who cannot afford adequate medical care, this represents a tough alternative because they certainly recognize the value of physical exams, immunizations, and other medical care.

SBC proponents often defend the clinics by arguing that few parents voice opposition to the clinic once they open. Three rejoinders readily come to mind. First, the failure to challenge the clinic may reflect the parents' sense of futility in fighting a *fait accompli*. A second possibility is that inner-city parents, probably preoccupied with keeping body and soul together, are either unwilling or unable to organize effective opposition to a clinic backed by the well-funded and powerful groups in the city. Third, opposition from parents is evident in south Chicago where two parents and twelve local ministers have filed a lawsuit to close down the local SBC in DuSable High School.

Reverend Arthur M. Brazier, pastor of the Apostolic Church of God—one of Chicago's largest Black churches—emphasized that when the school board establishes the school clinics that they "are, in effect, publicly announcing that they have given up hope for improvement in the morality of black youths" (Shipp 1985, 26).

The school board and other parties being sued attempted to have the case dismissed without going to trial, but the judge refused. The litigation is expected to drag on for months, and in the meantime the clinics remain in operation.

Washington, D.C.

In the nation's capital, Black community leaders and parents responded strongly against initial proposals to open a clinic that offered "reproductive health care services" in the Anacostia section of the city. At the initial public meeting held on December 11, 1985 to test public sentiment, parents and ministers from the area were almost unanimously opposed to the project on three grounds (Wagner 1986, 7-8). First, the SBC would undercut parental rights. Second, the local Planned Parenthood affiliate would operate the clinic. And third, the clinic's operating policies would promote immorality.

Thomas Held, a clinic supporter and teacher in the school where the clinic would be located, suggested another possible motive for opposition. According to a story in a local newspaper, the community may be skeptical of the clinic promoters because, Held said, it sees them, as "outsiders wanting to dump another program on them" (Allegar 1985).

The school board retrenched, let the opposition subside, and came back in March 1987 with a new proposal to offer the same type of clinic.[1] Planning for the SBCs continues, and whatever the outcome of this latest round of debate, it is clear that the school board and the mayor refuse to let the issue die, despite the parents' protest.

New York City

When the news broke in October 1986 about the unauthorized clinics in New York City, one of the most newsworthy facets of the controversy was the opposition of Black community leaders, who were suspicious about the fact "that the nine high schools with the state-financed health clinics were exclusively in minority areas," reported the *New York Times*, (Perlez 1986a, B8).

A noted Black educator, Donald H. Smith, professor of education at the City University of New York's Baruch College, told *Education Week* that the clinics "may be part of a movement to 'curtail the black birth rate and control the population' " (Viadero 1986, 1). Professor Smith is a past president of the National Alliance of Black Educators.

In addition, the New York Alliance of Black School Educators asked city officials why the clinics operated in predominantly minority areas. "If it's so wonderful, why wasn't it in Carnarsie? Why not Sheepshead Bay," asked Shelia Evans, president of the group in an article in *Education Week* (Viadero 1986, 12).

Other Black Leaders Speak Out

Other Black leaders from around the country have spoken out against SBCs. *Education Week* reported how in September 1986, Jack E. Robinson, Jr., then president of the Boston chapter of the N.A.A.C.P., "called a proposal to establish four school clinics there 'an experiment in social engineering.'" He resigned after the organization's executive board "took issue with his statements on the matter," observed the article (Viadero 1986, 6 and 12).

Rod Doss, editor of the *New Pittsburgh Courier*, one of the country's foremost Black newspapers, strongly denounced the plans of the school board's blue-ribbon task force, whose ultimate goal was the establishment of SBCs (Doss 1986, 1). "Once again, the black community has been targeted for control," Doss stated emphatically, "decimation and ultimately the destruction of the black family traditions and black life." Another Black journalist and author of a nationally syndicated column, William Raspberry, has come out in opposition to clinics (Raspberry 1986).

Conclusion

In promoting enactment of legislative measures such as the Hyde Amendment restricting government funding of abortions, right-to-life supporters have learned to cooperate with those who may oppose pro-abortion initiatives for different reasons, such as being unwilling to have their tax money used to pay for abortions.

This strategy carries over into the policy debates over school clinics very well. In the battle to stop SBCs, pro-lifers may also be able to find allies who are not anti-abortion or in favor of parental rights, but who take issue with the clinics for other financial, political, and ideological considerations. As we shall see in the next chapter, building a coalition of individuals and groups who oppose SBCs for a variety of reasons has proven to be the most effective way to combat school clinics.

CHAPTER EIGHT

LOCAL OPPOSITION STOPPING CLINIC PROPOSALS

"Our future is bright," proclaimed SBC expert Sharon Lovick during her speech closing the Center for Population Options' third national school-clinic conference in October 1986 (Lovick 1986). In view of the impressive growth in the number of the SBCs, it would seem hard to disagree.

However, as we have seen throughout this book, clinic advocates are now encountering serious opposition. A number of considerations, most specifically the promotion by SBCs of abortion counseling and referrals, and their undermining of parental authority, are stirring up grassroots resistance. Coalitions of opponents have turned back proposals to open SBCs in cities of all sizes across the country: Cincinnati; San Diego; Boston; Dayton, Ohio; Portland, Maine (the largest city in the state); Taylor, Michigan; and Meriden, Connecticut (Right to Life Ed. Foundation 1986; Reynolds 1986, B1; Hernandez 1987, 1; Madison 1986, 1; Coughlan 1987a; Prater 1987; Conley 1987, 1). In addition, stiff resistance has delayed, or even postponed, consideration of clinics in many other cities, including Los Angeles, Sacramento, and Miami (Moreland 1987, 1; Fallon 1986; Silva 1987, 1A).

This chapter describes the strategies that pro-life supporters have used to achieve these notable victories and then examines how SBC advocates have attempted to either circumvent or neutralize opposition to school clinics.

Four Pro-Life Strategies Capitalize on SBC Weaknesses

As well as SBC advocates have done during the past four years, their operations still have several major structural weaknesses to overcome if SBCs are to stay in business permanently. Three shortcomings seem to stand out: the inability of school-clinic proponents to demonstrate that SBCs reduce pregnancy, the possibility of a backlash when parents and the public learn how they have been duped about the SBCs' true nature, and uncertainties about stable sources of long-term funding.

Capitalizing on these weaknesses turns on using the same strategies that has been successful in fighting abortion. During workshops at the 1987 National Right to Life Convention, speeches by three well-informed and articulate right-to-lifers illustrated the rapidly growing sophistication of the anti-SBC forces. Ed Hurlbutt, executive director of United for Life in Fresno, California, an affiliate of the California Pro-Life Council; Jackie Schwietz, co-executive director of Minnesota Citizens Concerned for Life; and Chris Coughlan, director of chapter development of Maine Right to Life, described how they used lobbying, media, and educational techniques to defeat clinic proposals by exploiting those weaknesses.

Four general conclusions about pro-life tactics can be drawn from the speeches at the convention. One of the cardinal pro-life beliefs—founded on almost two decades of experience—is that the truth wins out in the end; therefore, *effective grassroots education is fundamental.* For example, with the abortion issue, when people look beyond the pro-abortion rhetoric and recognize the truth about the humanity of the child in the womb, they usually back away from supporting abortion. Often they join the pro-life ranks.

Likewise, with SBCs "the basic task we have is education," asserted Hurlbutt, during a workshop devoted to fighting SBCs conducted at the National Right to Life convention in New Orleans in June 1987 (Hurlbutt 1987). Hurlbutt has had extensive experience opposing SBCs. Pro-life advocates should actively encourage the public and policymakers to learn what SBC proponents plan to do in the clinics. "We have no reason to fear generating all the publicity, getting out all the information we can about the clinics, about their implications, about their failure," Hurlbutt asserted.

Another well-tested method to give pro-lifers and their allies an edge is to fight out the SBC issue at the local level. The closer to the people that policymakers—such as school board or city council members—are, the more responsive they are to their constituents' concerns.

All three speakers also emphasized the importance of maintaining a calm and rational approach to the policymakers during all phases of dealing with the SBC issue. Hurlbutt noted that quiet, informal discussions with school board members in four cities in his state had convinced them to oppose the clinics. The policymakers realized that they had been misled about the alleged efficacy of the SBC program. Hurlbutt cited the value of maintaining good relations with school board members, even those who might initially favor the clinics.

The final lesson evident in the reports of successful efforts to turn back SBCs that were presented at the NRL convention is the essential need to build coalitions effectively. Such coalitions have the capability to frame the terms of the debate and rally the voters to influence policymakers. Two reasons explain why right-to-life groups should work closely with other anti-SBC groups. Membership in a coalition gives the local right-to-life group a strong voice against SBCs without sacrificing its credibility as a single-issue organization. (Pro-life leaders who are trying to stop SBCs must constantly look to the long-term, always keeping in mind that the members of their group joined specifically because of their opposition to abortion, infanticide, and euthanasia. Coalition-building can *never* be undertaken at the expense of blurring the pro-life movement's single-issue focus. It is appropriate and useful to form coalitions; however, right-to-life supporters should focus *strictly* on the pro-life dimension of SBCs—how they promote and facilitate abortion.)

A coalition is also valuable because the larger and more diverse the group opposing the clinic, the more likely it is to succeed. An effective coalition demonstrates that a broad cross section of the community is against the SBC.

We should note that if there has been one redeeming factor in the spread of SBCs, it has been the boost it has given to building bridges between community groups that should be natural allies in the battle against abortion. There is a clear commonality of purpose of protecting our kids from the influence of SBCs and preventing our schools and our tax dollars from being used as a tool to undermine family and community values.

One excellent sign of this is the emergence around the country of a broad base of religious leaders who are stepping forward to oppose clinics. On the evangelical side, there is Dr. James Dobson, the well-known psychologist and family counselor, who made SBCs the cover story on the October, 1986 issue of his magazine *Focus on the Family*, and Dobson also devoted two parts of his national radio program to this pressing issue (Dobson 1986; Yorkey 1986, 2-5). Roman Catholic bishops in San Diego, Los Angeles, New York City, Boston, Miami, and other cities took the lead in denouncing SBCs, and the 300 members of the National Conference of Catholic Bishops unanimously approved a statement on November 17, 1987 strongly objecting to the establishment of school-based clinics on both moral and practical grounds (Lindquist and Reynolds 1986; Bernstein 1986; Perlez 1986e, B1; Hernandez 1987; Berger 1986; Overman 1987, 17; *Origins* 1987, 432-441). And Black pastors, such as the Reverend Hiram Crawford in Chicago and the Reverend Willie Wilson in Washington, D.C., have taken a leading role in local fights against opening the clinics (see Chapter Eight).

Despite the advantages SBC advocates usually enjoy in favorable publicity and access to policymakers, coalitions of citizen's groups with right-to-lifers playing key roles have stopped clinics in Cincinnati, Ohio; San Diego, California; Portland, Maine; Meriden, Connecticut; Taylor, Michigan; and at the state level in Missouri.

Recognizing and Countering School-Clinic Advocates' Tactics

Now that we have examined the methods that pro-lifers and other members of their coalitions have used to defeat SBCs, we turn our attention to the customary ways that pro-SBC advocates have won acceptance for their proposals in the past. Then we will look at the changes they have made in light of the growing opposition. According to Hurlbutt, efforts to establish a SBC generally follow a definite progression beginning with the initial activities to build community interest in opening a SBC and culminating with the clinic open and operating. The four phases of the pattern are:

- creating the "need" for the SBC;
- lobbying for passage of a specific proposal;
- activities when the SBC has been approved, but not funded;
- and an open and operating facility.

This section reviews what school-clinic advocates typically do at each step and then explores some of the possible ways that opponents can thwart those plans.

Phase One: *Creating the "Need" for a School Clinic*

The rapid growth of school-based clinics during the last three years was not an accident but the result of a carefully orchestrated campaign. The opening phase of the four-phase effort typically takes place well before any formal announcement of specific local plans to open a SBC. Savvy school-clinic advocates are adept at employing techniques designed to mobilize public opinion and the government bureaucracy behind the establishment of SBCs before the larger community has any idea that plans are in the offing.

Proponents capitalize, for example, on their excellent access to community leaders and to the print and electronic media to heighten public awareness of social and medical problems among adolescents, especially inner-city teenagers. The so-called "epidemic of teen pregnancy" has been the favorite theme.

One of the most noticeable trends among newspapers and television stations during the 1980s has been the growing emphasis on human-interest stories. Put this together with the metaphor of the "epidemic" of teen pregnancy and you have the recipe for the kind of stories sure to promote SBCs.

Typically, the account exploring teen pregnancies begins with a heartrending description of the travails of an unmarried teenaged girl whose life is portrayed as being marred, if not ruined, by an unexpected pregnancy and birth. The reporter used this attention-grabber to stress the high personal and societal costs of teen pregnancy. While perhaps not betraying too much boosterism for local SBCs, the journalist often quoted staff members (and other "experts") from SBCs in St. Paul or other cities who extoll the virtues of their facility in allegedly "helping" teens prevent pregnancies. Since these claims are taken at face value, the stories provide only a superficial analysis of how the SBC can ameliorate the teen pregnancy problem and rarely inquire whether SBCs in fact do reduce the incidence of teen pregnancy (Wallis 1985, 78; Carreau 1986; Dickey 1986, 1B; Flanery 1986, 1; Stephen 1986).

In some cities, the pre-clinic publicity campaign has taken another form. Advocates used public service and paid advertisements to set the stage for local SBC advocacy efforts. For example, Planned Parenthood and the Children's Defense Fund have run extensive and expensive advertising campaigns all over the country for the purpose of raising the visibility and public consciousness about teenage pregnancy. (See Chapter Three.)

SBC proponents commonly also arranged for the appointment of a city-wide task force by the major or city council to examine the teen-pregnancy issue and then came back to policymakers with specific recommendations as another way to generate momentum (i.e., Brandon 1986, 11; Regan 1986, A1; Fitzgerald 1986). (This process may start in this initial phase and then carry over into the next phase when policymakers are actively considering adoption of proposals to open a SBC).

Although the advisory committee may try to convey the impression that it is open to community input from all points of view, experiences in San Diego, Miami, Philadelphia, Cincinnati, Indianapolis, Baltimore, and Boston reveal that these "blue-ribbon" advisory committees are usually stacked with clinic supporters, who come equipped with a predetermined agenda—to recommend opening SBCs. In fact, the Mayor's Taskforce in Alexandria, Virginia even included the director of a for-profit abortion chamber, who also operated a teen clinic near the only high school in the city (Hernandez 1987, 19; Hicks 1986, 1-2; *San Diego Union* 1986; Fitzgerald 1986; Katz 1986, 2A; Center for Pop. Options 1986c, 4; Thomas 1987, 1; Kevin Cook 1986, 28).

During the task force's deliberations, parents and members of the public are allowed to speak, but often not until the skids have been greased making approval more likely. For example, the group appointed by the mayor of Minneapolis, a well-known abortion supporter, sponsored lectures and surveyed adolescents with a questionnaire that many parents found "abominable," reported Jackie Schwietz. "Many of the parents didn't know [the task force member] were doing it [administering the survey]," she explained, "and found out after the fact" (Schwietz 1987). Shutting out critics and establishing an "ad hoc" committee supportive of SBCs was effective in Minneapolis. The clinic was approved and opened.

However, such high-handed tactics can backfire. Even the pro-clinic media may turn around and eventually become more objective if they recognize how SBC advocates stifle public debate and subvert the democratic process. For example, the television and radio media in Los Angeles who had been skeptical of the clinic opponents, reported Hurlbutt, are beginning to change their perception of what is going on. They realized, he said, that the "school board intended to push these clinics through no matter what the parents and the citizens of the district wanted" (Hurlbutt 1987).

SBC Advocates Work
Behind The Scenes

One strategy used to set up the initial clinics, which is still effective in many places, is to keep the process of opening the clinic as quiet as possible and out of the public eye until the last moment before a vote.

Douglas Kirby recommended in 1985, "try to keep a low profile" (Kirby 1985, 21). The nation's oldest clinic, in Dallas, Texas, opened in 1970 "very quietly," pointed out Bill Price, president of the Greater Dallas Right to Life in a story in the *Washington Post* (Fisher 1987, A1). "The fact that it was done in a minority school enabled them to slip it in," he observed, "[a]nd the evangelical Christian community here wasn't geared up then to oppose it." In New York City, the SBC advocates were so secretive about the clinics that the school administration was very embarrassed in October 1986 once the newspapers revealed that nine SBCs were operating in the city without the knowledge and approval of the members of the school board. Some of the clinics had even been operating for as long as two years before the newspapers broke the story (Perlez 1986b, E6; 1986g, A1).

A related method that SBC proponents have utilized successfully to avoid controversy is extensive planning and coordination with school administrators, public health officials, and potential financing sources *before* any proposals to open a school clinic are announced publicly (O'Connor 1985, 1 and 6; Cathey 1987; Robinson 1986).[1] Thus, they are able to come forward with a well-thought-out proposal at the appropriate moment. This arrangement also provides SBC advocates ample opportunity to marshall their grassroots supporters to promote the clinics, while undercutting their critics who have little time to organize (Gauntt 1986; Belka 1986). For example, in Chicago and Portland, Oregon, the school board voted to open the clinics on very short notice, which did not allow the parents and right-to-lifers much time to mobilize (O'Connor 1986; Belka 1986).

However, this covert activity may work against the clinic proposal if SBC opponents can obtain access to the minutes of meetings and pertinent correspondence and expose the collusion, as they did in San Diego. In that case, the pro-lifers obtained the records under California's "sunshine law" which ensures that citizens can maintain a watchful eye over their government officials by obtaining copies of correspondence and notes of meetings (Hurlbutt 1987).

Since the nationwide press coverage in September 1985 about the Chicago SBCs, parents and community leaders have become more vigilant about the possible attempts to open SBCs in their schools. As a result, school-clinic advocates have found that the backdoor approach to opening clinics without arousing opposition is no longer as successful as it once was.

During this period before public announcement of plans to open a SBC, critics of SBCs should focus on primarily two activities—education and lobbying, suggested Ed Hurlbutt. First, "do a thorough study yourself," he suggested, "educate yourself; start to educate other people; especially find out if there is anything going [on]" (Hurlbutt 1987).

Another important lesson evident from the battles over the clinics in San Diego, Boston, Portland, Maine, and Alexandria, Virginia, is the importance of having right-to-life supporters participate in the "blue-ribbon" study committee process, if for no other reason than to keep informed of the proponents' activities. This offers the opportunity to ensure that important facts and opinions are placed on the record where they can be used later when SBCs come up for a vote. Pro-life members of the task force studying clinics in San Diego issued a devastating minority report critical of SBCs which formed the basis for the eventual rejection of the clinic by the school board (Hurlbutt 1987; Hicks 1986).

Keeping SBC critics up-to-date should also be a high priority. Since most of the media is likely to be favorably disposed to setting up SBCs, both Hurlbutt and Coughlan stressed the importance of finding and using alternative means of communication, including mailings of newsletters and other materials, telephone calls, letters to the editor, and literature distribution at churches (Hurlbutt 1987, Coughlan 1987).

Other avenues of education such as meetings and electronic media are also important, if they are available. For example, in Portland, Maine, the pro-life group kept its members informed through its newsletter, Coughlan said, and "we communicated to the general public basically by a Christian radio show" (Coughlan 1987a). Opponents of a SBC in Alexandria, Virginia, who organized under the name "Concerned Alexandrians for Responsible Education

(CARE)," placed a series of paid radio ads on a commercial station in an effort to generate support for its position (Clardy 1987, B3).

Another important information-gathering task is to inquire what counseling and referral policies are currently in place for pregnant girls in each of the city's secondary schools that do not have SBCs. Pro-lifers in Pennsylvania and New York were dismayed to learn that the school nurses and guidance counselors already routinely referred girls for abortion without parental knowledge or consent.

In addition to being well-informed and educating others, Hurlbutt suggested that opponents of SBCs at this juncture take the offensive by lobbying their local legislators and school board members in advance to forestall later approval of a school-clinic (Hurlbutt 1987). A coalition of groups may be able to push the local school board to go on record against school-based clinics. Such a board vote places the burden on SBC proponents by forcing them to convince the board members to overturn their previous action.

Phase Two:
Proposals Announced and Lobbying Begins

Once policymakers in the school board or city council begin to give serious consideration to opening a SBC, the process has entered the second of four stages. During this period, the subtleties of the opening phase when the proponents attempted to manipulate public opinion gives way to a full-scale public-policy debate in which both advocates and opponents use traditional lobbying techniques to mobilize support for their respective positions.

In order to avoid—or need be, overcome—anti-SBC opposition at this stage, clinic advocates have generally utilized any of four methods; sometimes they use only one, but, more frequently, all are employed together.

SBC Advocates Defame Critics
and Discredit Their Questions

SBC advocates have adopted two tried-and-true tactics historically used by pro-abortion supporters to deflect pro-life inquiries: attack the motives of the questionners and characterize their questions as either trivial or unworthy of consideration.

At the annual national SBC conference in October 1986, a speech by Joy Dryfoos exemplified both. First, she belittled the clinic "detractors" by characterizing them as "moralizers" who "have a field day of sermonizing, handwringing, trying to keep us off of their moral turf" (Dryfoos 1986c).[2] Then

Dryfoos described her resentment that SBC proponents "are being hard pressed on every side to generate data to prove scientifically that clinics work—that they prevent pregnancy" and so forth (Dryfoos 1986c). These requirements seemed unreasonable, in her opinion, since "the school-based clinic movement is being asked to justify itself in a much greater degree that most programs that I know about."

As an example, she cited the current substance-abuse prevention programs where millions of dollars are being spent without sufficient proof, in her opinion, that the efforts will achieve the desired results (Dryfoos 1986c). (Her objection ignores, of course, three fundamental differences between the SBCs and the initiatives among teens against drunk driving and substance abuse. The latter programs are almost entirely educational, promote abstinence and rehabilitation to get to the root cause of the problem, and are not nearly as invasive of the school environment as comprehensive health clinics.)

SBC proponents often imply, when they do not declare outright, that SBC critics are insensitive to the health problems of inner-city minority teens. The clear implication, of course, is that critics are callous, if not racist bigots, whose misgivings do not have to be taken seriously.

An article in the February 16, 1987 issue of *Newsweek* magazine provides an example (Kantrowitz 1986, 58). After describing the political opposition to clinics in Boston growing out of financial, social, moral considerations, the story pointed out that "[o]ften, the clinics provide the only medical care the kids get." Moreover, the current director of the DuSable clinic in Chicago told the magazine that "family planning is only one of 10 health programs— including regular examinations and prenatal care."

The reader is subtly led from one thought into another. Resistance to the clinic emanating from a narrow but important range of concerns over such issues as abortion is unfairly characterized as a broad attack on the whole health-care program. Opposition to SBCs becomes equivalent to indifference, or perhaps even callousness, toward minority students who would use the clinic. Only narrow-minded bigots, imply the SBC proponents, would jeo- pardize a vitally needed medical program because of one distasteful aspect.

This inaccurate and unfair characterization enables SBC advocates to assume the moral high ground in the debate and puts critics of the clinics on the defensive. Not only do opponents have to fight to be heard on the substan- tive issues they have been trying to raise in the first place, but their whole effort is also tainted with unearned bad associations.

Despite suggestions from a few SBC proponents that the school clinics should be evaluated objectively on their merits—rather than not abusing opponents rhetorically—critics of clinics continued to be assailed and their motives questioned. And why not? Critics have been so discredited in the eyes of many in the media that they are seldom, if ever, given a fair opportunity to present their alternative solutions to the inner-city teens health problems. That notwithstanding, the evidence is growing that school board and city council members for a change are beginning to take parental and community concerns more seriously for a change. Hopefully criticisms of SBCs will begin to be evaluated objectively.

Preventing Restrictions
on Abortion-Related Activity

During the intense jockeying and debate over a SBC proposal that takes place during the second phase, school-clinic supporters will use different approaches to protect themselves from serious restrictions on their abortion-related activities. Three stand out.

Although SBC advocates typically downplay the extent of a school-clinic's controversial services, they are absolutely unwilling to entertain any possibility of dropping them, or even consider providing them in a different location. For example, "[c]are related to reproductive health accounts for less than 25% of the total monthly services provided by SBCs," reported the Center for Population Option's "The School-Based Clinic Update 1987," "and a number of programs provide relatively little in the area of reproductive health care" (Lovick 1987c, 8). "However, program operators consider these services to be important to the clinic operation," continued the report, and 80% of the respondents to the survey of 47 programs operating 85 separate clinics believe that such services "are an essential part of clinic services."

Likewise, Terrance Keenan, vice president of the Robert Wood Johnson Foundation, defended his organization's $16.8 million grant program financing SBCs that offer the reproductive health services. The *Foundation News* reported that he said that "the foundation has no intention of dropping the controversial parts of the AHP [School-Based Adolescent Health] program" (*Foundation News* 1987, 13).

The reason that the controversial services are so "essential," say SBC advocates, is that they reduce teen pregnancies. However, the proponents are unable to support those contentions with hard statistics and have elevated dodging embarrassing questions about the lack of evidence to an art form. As analyzed in detail in chapter five, clinic proponents have successfully convinced policymakers to accept inadequate statistical data and meaningless measures of effectiveness.

Another common approach used by SBC staff and supporters to fend off the opposition is to employ half-truths, especially when it comes to abortion. SBC proponents realize that if clinics are linked to abortion it can amount to a "kiss of death." The issue is so controversial that most politicians do not want to have anything to do with it. No matter what position politicians take, they feel that they will end up alienating some group in the community (Katz 1986, 2).

In order to placate concerned legislators and worried parents, the school-clinic advocates strongly assert that the clinic will not perform abortion counseling and referrals. They are even initially willing to accept nominal restrictions on counseling and *direct*1 referrals to abortion providers because they know they can accomplish the same objective by performing *indirect* referrals instead. If the issue of abortion counseling or referrals comes up after the clinic has already opened, the staff will claim that the clinic does not offer that service. Often this half-truth appeases the politicians, who unfortunately fail to clarify what kinds of activity the staff was talking about—direct or indirect referrals, or both.

Judith Steinhagen, principal of the DuSable High School clinic in south Chicago, illustrated how this tactic is used during her interview on the *MacNeil-Lehrer News Hour* on November 24, 1986 (MacNeil/Lehrer 1986). In response to the observation by the TV correspondent that the leader of the clinic's opposition, the Reverend Hiram Crawford, was said to have said that pregnant girls are referred by the DuSable clinic to local hospitals for abortions, Steinhagen responded strongly "That's a lie. That's a lie." However, when the reporter probed more deeply about how the clinic staff actually handles pregnant girls, Steinhagen acknowledged that some girls from her school had obtained abortions; but she asserted that "those referrals are not made by the school nor the clinic." Unfortunately, the reporter let her off of the hook by failing to ask about the DuSable clinic's indirect abortion-referral activities.

Steinhagen's denial about doing abortion referrals, of course, only told half the story. DuSable's clinic utilizes the same policies as the Orr High School clinic, which is not surprising since both are controlled by the same organization—the Ounce of Prevention Fund (Banas 1986, 4). And, as we have seen in Chapter Two, the nurse practitioner from Orr readily stated in private that his clinic performs indirect abortion referrals. Therefore, DuSable's staff may not perform *direct* abortion referrals; however, the staff will arrange for an *indirect* referral by sending the pregnant girl to an agency outside of the school, which in turn directs her to an abortionist.

In the event that the clinic proposal seems doomed to defeat because of recalcitrance about abortion-related services, experienced SBC advocates recommend in the short run sacrificing all of the controversial features in order to accomplish the major goal—getting the facility opened inside of the school. "Be willing to make compromises," recommended Kathleen Arnold-

Sheeran, former staff member of the St. Paul program (quoted in Patton 1986a). "Better something than nothing." The point she was making was "[d]o not compromise on being in school." The controversial services that were not included initially can always be added later, as they were in Kansas City, she said. In Michigan, Paul Shaheen adopted the same philosophy very effectively: "We took what we could get at that moment, and then moved on to get some more" (Shaheen 1986).

Building Pro-SBC
Grassroots Support

Faced with growing local resistance to school-based clinics during public debates, SBC advocates apparently have decided that they must supplement their "top down" strategy by building their own strong group of local supporters within each community. Perhaps they took their cue from pro-life electoral and legislative successes which have depended in large measure on having a strong grassroots organization in place.

A substantial portion of the comprehensive manual published in September 1986 by the Center for Population Options, titled *School-Based Health Clinics: A Guide To Implementing Programs*, was devoted to detailed instructions on developing a core group of supporters within the community. The *Guide* especially emphasized gaining adherents in the area where the SBC is likely to be located. SBC proponents should press for development of a "Community Advisory Board" as a "formal symbol of community support," stated the *Guide*. With this purpose in mind, it would make sense for advocates to follow Douglas Kirby's recommendation (as noted in chapter six) that the committee "[i]nclude only people basically supportive of the idea" (Kirby 1985, 19).

During this crucially important period when community leaders are deliberating about SBCs, pro-lifers have learned through hard-won experience that they must work diligently (and frequently on short notice) to mobilize resistance to opening school clinics in their communities. SBC critics can often point out the unfair and biased process that is being used to railroad approval of SBCs through the school board or city council.

Continuing the educational efforts against the clinics—begun during stage one to counter the groundwork that SBC proponents were laying at the time—is also essential. One of the top initial priorities for pro-lifers and their allies as soon as any announcement is made about plans being placed before the school board or city council to open a SBC is to ascertain specific information about the proposed SBC's policies and activities. Once that is accomplished, critics will able to compare what the local SBC proponents are saying with the published accounts about how clinics are operated elsewhere.

Exposing the adverse social, moral, and financial impacts of SBCs has proven to be a key to defeating plans. According to Ed Hurlbutt, Joan Patton, leader of the successful struggle against SBCs in San Diego, "got into every forum that she could in order to educate people about the function, the purpose, the implications, and the failures of these clinics" (Hurlbutt 1987). By demanding answers to tough questions about all facets of the proposed clinic's operations, critics, such as Patton, can force advocates and staff members to go on record on matters, such as abortion, that they would rather leave untouched.

The evidence about how the facility will undercut parents and promote abortion can overcome indifference and stimulate development of the key elements of building coalitions to prevent establishment of school clinics. For example, the majority of the votes cast against the clinic proposal in San Diego and Cincinnati was based on pro-life and pro-family objections about SBCs. However, in both San Diego and Cincinnati, other criticisms helped sway the board member who cast the decisive vote against the proposal. In one case it was because of financial considerations, and in the other, the member's worries about overburdening the schools.

And finally, if it appears that the SBC may possibly be approved, opponents should try to restrict the operations as tightly as possible. Moreover, critics should demand that policymakers set a definite time in the future when the SBC would be evaluated by an independent and objective authority to ascertain whether it had met its goals. Such an evaluation should be conducted and announced publicly *prior* to a vote for refunding. This step is especially important if the school board or city council have predicated establishing the SBC on the expectation that it will reduce pregnancies among students in that school. Statistics about pregnancy tests and abortion referrals could be very enlightening. And, as noted in Chapter Five, the staff will almost certainly be unable to produce reliable data demonstrating that the SBC reduced teen pregnancies. Perhaps at that juncture, opponents will have an opportunity to close down the school clinic.

Third Stage:
SBC Accepted, But Not Funded

If, despite lobbying and educational efforts against a school-based clinic, local policymakers decide to establish a SBC, opponents should not lose heart. The process of setting up a SBC has moved into a third stage, and the struggle is by no means over. Hurlbutt pointed out that an affirmative vote does not necessarily mean that the SBC will open. It still must be funded. And since such facilities are very expensive, the local government or other backers may not be able to find the financing. Opponents can keep up the pressure to stop the facility all during this third stage.

Hurlbutt cited the example of Sacramento where the clinic approved by the county board of supervisors has not received any financial support (Hurlbutt 1987; McGrath 1987). Likewise, in Los Angeles, after one SBC opened, opponents delayed the funding process for two others by initiating a letter-writing campaign and even renting an airplane-pulled advertising banner in an effort to discourage the Robert Wood Johnson Foundation from putting any money into them (Hurlbutt 1987; Moreland 1987).

Unfortunately, the Foundation eventually did decide in July 1987 to fund those facilities (Center for Pop. Options 1987), but that did not prove that the tactic is ineffective. In December 1986, local resistance in Paterson, New Jersey caused the Foundation to drop plans to finance a SBC there (Berger 1986).

In July 1987, the Johnson Foundation withdrew its $600,000 grant to a proposed clinic in Miami, Florida when Governor Bob Martinez indicated that the state government did not support the facility (Silva 1987, 1A). Proponents are attempting to salvage the funding by identifying a non-profit, non-governmental agency to reapply for the grant to operate the SBC (Center for Pop. Options 1987c, 6).

Fourth Stage: Continued Resistance to An Open and Operating Facility

The fourth stage of clinic development is when the SBC is already open and operating. Continuing effective resistance may appear to be difficult because critics will find that the controversial services provided by the SBC may be harder to keep in the public eye. However, Hurlbutt observed that SBC opponents have kept up the pressure by stressing how the clinic is a threat to family integrity, especially through its activity as an abortion referral center (Hurlbutt 1987). This may even discourage students from visiting it.

Another idea, which parents and community leaders adopted in Chicago when all of their other recourses were exhausted, is to file a lawsuit against the SBC. This is a very costly and lengthy process. A far better approach is to influence policymakers to never allow the clinic to open in the first place.

Persistent Opposition

Pro-lifers must never give up even if the clinic is voted in; the fight is never over. Certainly the proponents of the clinics do not see the vote as the final word.

Just because the clinic is voted down, do not assume the proponents are going to drop the proposal, Hurlbutt said (Hurlbutt 1987). After the defeat of the clinic in San Diego in July 1986 by a narrow 3 to 2 vote, one of the leading supporters immediately ran for the school board. Despite spending $90,000, the SBC advocate lost by a narrow margin. The moral of the story, Hurlbutt said, is that "you have to think that you are going to get in it for the long run."

Advocates' New Strategy to Leapfrog or Neutralize Opposition

State-Level Initiatives to Bypass Local Opposition

While the stages just outlined represent the way SBC proponents typically get their proposals adopted, they have reevaluated their methods and made some changes in response to mounting opposition. Speeches at several conferences provide some clues to the new methods they may use in the coming months to circumvent or neutralize opposition.

Some clinic advocates are modifying their strategies in ways roughly analogous to what they did years ago in the campaign to legalize abortion nationwide. The overall objective is to shift control of the decision-making process to the level of government on which pro-lifers and their allies have the least direct influence.

In the case of abortion, the pro-abortion lobby, having initially gone to the state legislatures, then turned to the federal courts to circumvent opposition that had developed from federal, state, and local elected officials. In 1973 the U.S. Supreme Court elevated abortion to a constitutional right by overturning laws restricting abortion in every state in the country.

In a similar way, leading pro-SBC spokesmen laid out definite plans at workshops at two national conferences in 1986 and 1987 for a coordinated strategy to use state-level legislation to "leapfrog" (our word, not theirs) community opposition to SBCs. Recent experiences in Congress and the states of Michigan, Minnesota, and Oregon—to name just a few—have shown that the SBC advocates seek to eliminate local authority to regulate the school clinics by passing state or federal laws which not only provide a financial incentive to start clinics, but also mandate that the SBCs follow certain policies.

When grassroots parental opposition appears too strong, clinic advocates will try to circumvent the local citizens by obtaining state-level funding. In Michigan, for example, Paul Shaheen explained that the members of his taskforce decided that "we don't think that each adolescent clinic should fight this battle on the community level." Remember, he pointed out to the clinic advocates, "if you can get it done at the state level, then you don't have to fight these battles alone" (Shaheen 1986). The growth in this type of initiatives, observed Jodie Levin-Epstein at a workshop on SBCs held in March 1986, is going to change the nature of school-based clinics. They are now going to be "top-down operations rather than bottom-up," she explained (Levin-Epstein 1986a). "The clear advantage of state investment in school-based clinics," in her opinion, "is continued funding." Equally significant, we would note, is that state-level control would give SBC staffers relative immunity from local opposition.

Despite the pro-SBC advocates' headstart at working on SBCs at a statewide level, critics have been quite successful in working with state officials to prevent SBCs from opening. As noted earlier, in July 1987, Governor Bob Martinez delayed the opening of a SBC in Miami, Florida by rejecting a $600,000 grant from the Robert Wood Johnson Foundation. The director of Missouri Department of Public Health announced in August 1987 that the state would not finance any new SBCs, "partly because of growing opposition to such projects," reported the *St. Louis Post-Dispatch* (Dine 1987, 1). As described in chapter four, Minnesota's state legislature turned down several proposals to fund SBCs during the 1987 legislative session (Schwietz 1987). Wisconsin Governor Tommie Thompson vetoed a $2 million appropriation for SBCs. The Illinois state legislature passed an anti-SBC measure to prohibit abortion counseling and referrals, but unfortunately the law was vetoed by Governor James Thompson (Center for Pop. Options 1987c, 6).

Turning to the Courts

Judging by twenty-two years of experience confronting Planned Parenthood and its pro-abortion allies, we can expect that if their plan to use the legislative branch to bypass local opposition does not work, they will very likely turn to the courts. In fact, at a conference in mid-1984, Alfred Moran, executive vice president of Planned Parenthood of New York City, pointed out to the audience of abortion providers that "if you look at the history of the reproductive health care movement in this country, you will be struck by the fact that reproductive rights. . . have not been endowed on us by the presidents of this country, by the Senate, by the Congress or by state legislators." "We have won each and every single right that we have with respect to reproductive freedom in this country," he continued, "out of a struggle to take cases to the United States Supreme Court" (Moran 1984).

Let us examine two, not-unlikely scenarios where the courts may step in to achieve for the school-based clinic advocates what they were unable to do on their own through the legislative process. One legal challenge could rely on federal constitutional grounds, and the other would depend on state law. Judging from their track record on abortion, the SBC proponents never intend to abide by decisions hammered out in the legislative arena because they readily turn to the courts to overturn them.

In one scenario, which could happen in any state, a SBC opens after the staff promises not to perform abortion counseling or referrals. But then a staff member (or perhaps a surrogate such as a teenaged girl in the school) files a lawsuit to require that the clinic provide those services on the basis that the failure to do so violates the staff's (or the teenager's) U.S. constitutional rights. (The grounds that pro-abortion advocates might use could include the counselor's guarantee of freedom of speech under the First Amendment to give information or the teenager's right to privacy under the Fourteenth Amendment.) The court agrees with the plaintiff and rules that the school board or local government cannot control that part of the clinic's operations. The clinic becomes an abortion counseling and referral center, which, for the most part, is indistinguishable from Planned Parenthood's community-based offices.

Another possible scenario arises in one of the thirty-two states where the state law permits Planned Parenthood and its pro-abortion allies to cut parents out of their child's decisions about "reproductive health care," including pregnancy tests and abortion counseling and referrals (Center for Pop. Options 1986a, 3). We can suppose, as in the first scenario, that initially the clinic staff accepts restrictions on their abortion-related services as a precondition for receiving approval for opening. However, someone challenges those policies in court on the grounds that they violate the state law requiring confidential treatment (that is, without parental knowledge or consent) of minors. Then the court invalidates the restrictions. Once again, this gives the clinic staff a free hand to operate as they had wanted to do all along.

Neither of these scenarios has occurred yet. Perhaps pro-abortion advocates will decide not to push the issue too hard for fear of aggravating local school or city officials, who would be upset if they lost their control of the school programs. Moreover, extenuating circumstances such as the body of law about school operations may cloud the issue enough that the pro-abortion advocates might not be guaranteed of victory.

Nevertheless, the possibility that the courts could strike down restrictions on abortion counseling and referrals presents a strong argument for stopping clinics before they open. Once the clinic is in the school, a court challenge could invalidate any restrictions.

Pro-SBC Leader
Summaries Current Thinking

Seldom do SBC critics receive a comprehensive overview of what the school-clinic advocates may be planning in the future. A speech on November 7, 1987 by Sharon Lovick, a leading professional SBC promoter with an unexcelled vantage point to survey the nationwide situation, summarized the current thinking of pro-SBC advocates (Lovick 1987b). Speaking at the conclusion of the final plenary session, titled "Building Community Consensus in the Face of Opposition," of the fourth annual SBC national conference in Kansas City, Missouri, Lovick expounded on "five rules for handling the opposition." She had gleaned these principles from two-and-a-half years of conducting training, providing technical assistance, and talking with SBC staff members around the country. Although aware that members of the opposition were in the audience, she was remarkably candid and direct. Some of her specific suggestions will quite likely crop up in local debates.

Lovick's first rule was "know the opposition." By this she meant finding out information about the personal lives of the leaders in order to accuse them of being interlopers who were trying to force their morality on other people. She suggested ascertaining "where do their children go to school?" "Nine out of ten times," Lovick asserted, "you'll find that those who are the most vocal in their opposition to the clinics don't even live in the community where the clinic is being considered or attend the school where it's going to be located." She also pointed out how a young person who testified against SBCs before a U.S. Senate committee in June 1987 was discredited as a witness, at least in Lovick's opinion, when she admitted that she had "never seen a school-based clinic, never been inside one."

This tactic of accusing critics of being "outsiders" is thoroughly consistent with the attempts by SBC advocates across the country to discredit their opponents and discount their questions. The lesson for pro-lifers in this case is plain: build a broad coalition of opposition to SBCs and be sure to include parents from the school targeted for the SBC. In addition, if SBC proponents take this tack, it may be important to remind policymakers and the public that the impetus for starting SBCs did not come from inner-city, economically disadvantaged parents, but from "outsiders," such as social or public health workers, school officials, or wealthy foundation bureaucrats. The obvious question which should be raised is: Do the people in the area really want school clinics or are SBCs being imposed on them by the power brokers in the community?.

Another facet of the strategy of "know the opposition" that "has been proven very successful in many communities," Lovick noted, has been to encourage parents, school-board members, and clergy to learn more about the clinic program. "Take'em to a clinic," she urged, because "[i]t's difficult to understand what happens there." She clearly anticipated that most of the community leaders and members of the public would not be informed enough to ask the penetrating questions that would rip away the facade disguising the clinic's abortion connection.

The Center for Population Option's staff member also urged the conference audience to "[f]ind out who you might think will be in the opposition." Get them involved in the planning process for the SBC "from the beginning, no matter how difficult it might be," she said emphatically. "Don't wait for somebody to come out against a clinic and then react." Why would she propose this? This technique can help neutralize most of the opposition, observed Paul Shaheen, one of the principal architects behind passage of state-level legislation in Michigan to establish 100 clinics. Speaking at a SBC workshop in 1986, he explained that a taskforce of over one hundred organizations studied teen pregnancy, and when the majority of the group reached a consensus and issued a report favorable to SBCs, the small faction critical of the school clinics appeared to be a mere "vocal minority"—out of touch with the mainstream thinking.

The second of Lovick's five rules is closely related to the first: understand the opposition's tactics. She totally mischaracterized both the motives and methods of SBC critics. Claiming that opponents use "the sensitive issue of teen sexuality" to disguise their hidden ideological and political agenda permits Lovick (and presumably other SBC advocates) to avoid addressing the basic objections to SBCs—their abortion counseling and referrals and undercutting parental rights—which should be raised and fully discussed in a public-policy debate. The implicit point that she is probably trying to make is the need to establish the terms of the debate: if the issue is how SBCs promote abortion—or violate parental rights—SBC supporters will be thrown on the defensive.

Lovick's third rule emphasized that SBC proponents should aggressively promote services dealing with teen sexuality and be prepared with "individualized answers" to the questions that would inevitably come up. "Do not apologize to the attention being placed on reproductive health within the context of comprehensive health-care programs," she urged. "That is socially and morally responsible," she said.

She also indirectly chastized school-clinic proponents who use the teen-pregnancy issue to attract public attention and support, but who back off from actually offering the controversial services when opposition arises. "In your efforts to push school-based clinics," stated Lovick, "don't use teenage pregnancy as your reason if you're not going to tackle the issue in a very real and aggressive way."

Lovick's stress on the importance of reproductive health services in this section of her speech contrasted sharply with the general tenor of the 1987 national SBC conference where those controversial issues were hardly mentioned. In fact, in opening the Kansas City meeting, Lovick announced that the principal subject of the sessions would be "mental health," such as counseling teenagers about depression and suicide.

Moreover, the inability of the SBC advocates to produce comprehensive statistics to support their assertions about the ability of SBCs to reduce teen pregnancy was especially evident at the Kansas City conference. None of the reports about on-going research at SBCs revealed any new data showing that the clinics could reduce pregnancies. Louise Kaegi, a leader of the opposition to SBCs in the Chicago area, who attended both the national SBC conference in Chicago in 1985 and the latest one in Kansas City, remarked at the change in emphasis between the two meetings. In Chicago, she noted, the proponents stressed how SBCs would turn the "epidemic of teen pregnancy" around, but in Kansas City there was hardly a mention of that issue (Kaegi 1987).

Interestingly, Lovick devoted only two sentences to explaining her rather unexceptionable and unnoteworty fourth rule: "Don't assume that all concerns are not legitimate."

Finally, she suggested in rule five that SBCs "document and report your program accomplishments on a routine basis." Yet, as noted in chapter five, that has not been the history. SBC advocates will very likely try to collect statistics showing that they enticed a large number of teens into their clinic, but the SBC staff will be unwilling to attempt to gather accurate data revealing the impact of the SBC on teen pregnancy.

Conclusion

Sharon Lovick's remarks summarizing the latest pro-SBC strategy to counter the opposition revealed that school-clinic proponents will continue to be remain steadfastly unwilling to debate openly the generating pro-life opposition to school-based clinics. Moreover, if they follow her lead, SBC proponents will be even more aggressive in trying to seize the offensive. They will attempt to establish their own agenda for the public-policy debate and recruit support from a broad spectrum of the community, especially from parents and leaders in the area where the school clinic would be located.

This response by SBC advocates indicates that pro-lifers and their allies must be doing something right. By emphasizing grassroots organization and education, coalition members have successfully prevented establishment of school clinics. Most members of the public will support the pro-lifers and their allies after learning the truth about proponents' actual objectives and the dangerous ramifications of exposing vulnerable teenagers to the clinic's programs.

CHAPTER NINE

AN UNCERTAIN
FUTURE FOR SBCS

For the reasons outlined in this book, current media reports of SBCs have drawn a grossly distorted picture of how SBC development is really proceeding in local communities. Caught up in the enthusiasm for what is advertised as a panacea for the rising number of teen pregnancies, the press has not yet picked up on the surge of opposition to SBCs spearheaded by right-to-lifers. In a sense, this oversight is understandable for it was not until late 1986 and early 1987 that the battle was joined. Thus, we may fairly conclude that the early victories rolled up by the pro-SBC forces offer no clue to their the future prospects, *provided* the inflated claims of SBC proponents are punctured and their real agenda exposed.

School-Clinic
Advocates Optimistic

At the third national conference on SBCs held in October 1986, SBC proponents were bursting at the seams with optimism. And why not? Business was booming, more clinic openings were eminent, and they could foresee in the not-so-distant future attaining a long-cherished goal: virtually unlimited, direct access to the minds and bodies of impressionable teenagers. In the speech opening the Denver meeting, Joy Dryfoos played to that optimism by placing their work in a broader perspective. "At the close of the first and second conferences," she said, "we asked ourselves: 'Is there a school-based clinic movement? Does the idea have long-term viability or is it just a fad?' " (Dryfoos 1986c). "It is my biased opinion," Dryfoos proclaimed, "that we can start this conference by acknowledging that this is a movement. The concept is feasible, and that we are slowing building accountability and in most parts of the country, there is broad support (Dryfoos 1986c)."

The pamphlet "School-Based Clinics: Update 1986," prepared especially for the SBC conference, offered support for Dryfoos' claims (Lovick and Wesson 1986, 1). The number of SBCs had increased from 23 facilities in

1984 to 61 in the summer of 1986—almost two hundred percent growth. During the three-day meeting, the sponsors of the conference were pleasantly surprised to learn that an additional ten more clinics existed. The number increased dramatic the following year, as the November 1987 edition of "The School-Based Clinic Update" listed 101 separate clinic sites in operation, with another 100 being planned (Lovick 1987c, 4).

Tactics Self-Defeating

Ironically, publicity about the SBC proponents' overblown claims of reducing teen pregnancy and their "successes" in opening new facilities may contribute to their eventual undoing in two ways.

SBCs' increased visibility both locally and nationally has brought with it heightened media and public interest. Being in the spotlight makes it difficult for clinic proponents to work quietly behind the scenes to manipulate the policy process.

In addition, since the nationwide publicity in September 1985 about the Chicago clinic, more right-to-life supporters and other clinic opponents have recognized the grave seriousness of the threat posed by SBCs. Opposition has begun to get organized.

This heightened scrutiny of SBCs probably signals the end of the period when clinic advocates are routinely able to open clinics virtually without challenge. More clinics will continue to open since many are well along in the planning process, but the days of "easy pickings" are over.

Broad Range of Issues Drives
Coalition Opposing School Clinics

Opposition to SBCs has coalesced around the strong reaction against the dangerous moral and social implications of placing the facilities in schools. As we saw in the previous chapter, three major pro-life criticisms have a track record of proven effectiveness in mobilizing public resistance.

School Clinics Cause More Abortions

First, as the careful critiques in Chapter Two have demonstrated, SBCs cause more—not fewer—abortions. SBC staff members steadfastly maintain a public facade of non-involvement in abortion counseling and referral but then talk and write among themselves about how to promote both direct and indirect abortion referrals.

Two types of SBCs perform confidential abortion counseling and referrals directly to abortionists: those receiving certain types of federal funds and those not explicitly prevented by local policymakers from being involved with abortion. When clinics operate under policies which prohibit direct referrals, the staff arranges for the pregnant teen to receive those services without parental knowledge and consent in a different way. The clinic sends the pregnant girl to an outside local agency—such as a family planning clinic— which will provide the services.

In order to minimize controversy, SBC advocates carefully "finesse" the abortion connection, to use Joy Dryfoos' apt description. As we saw in Chapters One and Two, SBC proponents employ several techniques to downplay this abortion linkage and hide their real agenda.

One approach for deflecting criticism, as mentioned above, is to deny direct involvement—which can be true—yet accomplish the same goal by referring indirectly. Another technique described in Chapter Three is to orchestrate the pro-SBC publicity and lobbying campaign under the guise of apparently disinterested and objective research.

The SBC advocates' third approach is to claim that the primary objective in promoting SBCs is not to further their own narrow pro-abortion agenda but to provide "comprehensive" medical services. However, as we saw in Chapter One, SBC proponent Sharon Lovick has revealed how this is a smokescreen for their real objective—"doing something about adolescent pregnancy." In fact, as explained in Chapter Four, operating clinics inside schools offers Planned Parenthood and its allies an unparalleled opportunity to accomplish four long-sought-after goals: use the close proximity to the students and the school's authority to control the teenagers' lives, counter pro-life gains among the youth, add new sources of income, and diversify their range of medical services.

Misleading Claims About Reducing Pregnancies

The right-to-lifers' second objection, as discussed in Chapter Five, is to the misleading—and often completely erroneous—claims that SBCs reduce the number of teen pregnancies. A thorough review of their own statistics reveals how the hype does not square with the reality. Data from pilot clinics in St. Paul, Baltimore, and Chicago are simply inadequate to support the many claims of success. SBCs may have been shown to reduce births, but that was achieved by *increasing* the number of abortions, not *decreasing* the number of pregnancies.

Undercutting Parents

As we discussed in Chapter Six, a third successful pro-life critique of clinics is their policy of providing medical services, including abortion counseling and referrals, behind parents' backs. Individuals and groups who might not otherwise be strongly motivated to speak out about the abortion connection have joined anti-SBC coalitions because they grasped how clinics thoroughly undercut parental authority and seriously undermined the integrity of the family.

Five Other Objections

In addition to these three key criticisms, opponents have raised other major objections, financial and moral, to clinics. Their financial considerations include questions about the high cost/low cost-effectiveness of the clinics; the inevitable requirement for government funding; and the need for extensive medical liability insurance coverage should cause policymakers to reject SBCs. In addition, many parents and other concerned citizens are justifiably worried that the clinics will overburden school systems which are barely able to achieve their fundamental educational mission now. And finally, critics have pointed out the racist implications of targetting the clinics almost exclusively for schools in inner-city minority neighborhoods.

Growing Criticism, Mounting Resistance

Pro-lifers battling clinics can take heart from a major lesson learned from fighting abortion over the past fifteen years: Planned Parenthood and its fellow travelers bring highly visible assets into the public policy debate; but the pro-life movement has significant resources which may not be as apparent. The pro-abortion forces won their victories legalizing abortion in the late 1960s and early 1970s with the help of millions of dollars from private foundations and with the assistance of the courts and the media.

Despite having very few financial resources and only a nascent organizational structure initially, right-to-life opposition prevented the pro-abortion movement from extending its influence over other key institutions in American society. For example, after the U.S. Supreme Court's 1973 *Roe v. Wade* decision legalized abortion on demand, grassroots resistance thwarted the abortion industry's attempts to subvert the nation's hospitals by turning them into mass destruction centers for thousands of unborn babies. While it is true that over 1,100 hospitals continue to perform abortions each year, 83% of the killing goes on in the free-standing facilities which the abortionists established when they found many hospitals unreceptive to performing hundreds, and even thousands, of abortions annually (Henshaw 1987, 67). In other words, if grassroots pro-life pressure had not prevented the pro-abortion movement from taking over that key national health institution, very likely abortion would be even more widespread than it already is, and more babies would be dying every year.

Likewise, since the late 1970s constituent pressure on Congress has virtually cut the abortion industry off from the federal Treasury and saved the lives of tens of thousands of unborn children each year. In both instances, mobilization of the right-to-life forces did not happen overnight. It required years of grassroots pro-life work educating, recruiting and building chapters of supporters. And it had a very positive effect.

During the mid-1980s, the pro-abortion advocates opened a new front. They attempted to move their abortion counseling and referral operations directly into the schools. Apparently dissatisfied with the ineffectiveness of their "sex education" and in-school visits in bending the wills of teenagers, they are seeking to utilize one of the most pervasive and influential institutions in American society to funnel a captive clientele into abortion chambers.

Successful campaigns mounted against SBCs in cities such as San Diego, Cincinnati, Boston, and Portland, Maine, demonstrate that the general public and elected officials will reject the school clinics when they recognize how they promote abortion and undermine parental rights. Critics have also been able to influence the debate significantly when they cleared away the smokescreens and revealed the truth hidden by the SBC advocates' deceptive tactics.

Even in areas where clinics were established before opposition became organized, pro-life supporters should not give up hope. Consistent educational efforts may yet generate enough public pressure to close a local SBC. (See chapter eight.)

By building well-organized coalitions and focusing on the terrible harm that SBCs can do, right-to-life supporters can mobilize to protect their junior and senior high school children from falling under the malevolent influence of school-based clinics. If past experience is any guide, the key to success is to provide the factual evidence and then rely on the American public's inherent common sense and strong interest in justice. When they recognize the truth about SBCs, many will join the right-to-life ranks and tip the scales in favor of life.

SBC Advocates Admit Clinics Fail to Reduce Teen Pregnancies

As we go to press, Douglas Kirby, director of research for the Center for Population Options (CPO), the major national organization promoting school-based clinics, announced in a speech delivered on March 2, 1988 that school-based clinics (SBCs) have had "no measurable impact" on teen pregnancy rates. This startling admission from one of the most influential leaders in the pro-SBC movement completely demolishes the principal justification that proponents of SBCs have used to open these facilities that promote abortion. In other words, the Center for Population Options' own research supports the principal thesis developed in Chapter Five: that there is no reason to believe that school-based clinics reduce the incidence of teenage pregnancy.

Kirby described this sensational finding during a report explaining the results of the Center for Population Options' three-year study of six representative school-based clinics around the country given at a workshop at the annual meeting of the National Family Planning and Reproductive Health Association in Washington, D.C.. Although he prefaced his comments during a speech on the "Effectiveness of School-Based Clinics" with the caveat that they had not "finalized" the results, Kirby stated that "I am reasonably confident that what I am going to say will hold true" when the final report is published in late summer or early fall, 1988.

Reading between the lines, one might perceive that the study did not support the conclusions that the Center for Population Options (CPO) would have wanted. To its credit, CPO apparently will not attempt to either suppress or discredit entirely its own study. Kirby offered some explanations why the study did not show that SBCs reduced teen pregnancies, but a fair reading of his reasons that the school clinics had too small an impact to measure all come down to the fact that no matter how much SBCs provide in services, it will never be enough. In other words, the proponents will not admit that their program is unsuccessful in achieving its goals for they believe that success is just "around the corner," if they could only make the program larger.

Despite the survey's apparently disappointing results, the Center for Population Options has not abandoned its promotion of SBCs. Judging from Kirby's comments at the workshop about other findings of the research project, CPO will no longer emphasize that SBCs can prevent teen pregnancy and instead adopt a different approach. For example, underscoring the provision of general health care to inner-city teens would be much less controversial.

Pro-life supporters may take heart in the fact the SBC proponents have finally conceded that school clinics are ineffective in reducing teen pregnancies. However, this development has no bearing on the two principal right-to-life objections to SBCs—their promotion of abortion and undermining of parental rights.

For text of Kirby's remarks see Chapter Nine endnote, page 125.

APPENDIX ONE

Statistics on Adolescent Pregnancy, Abortion, Births, and Miscarriages

The analysis of adolescent pregnancies and abortions in the Introduction is based in large measure on the following tables of statistics about adolescent pregnancies, abortions, births, and miscarriages. The tables display the same data in different ways.

The sources are listed at the end of each table. As discussed in detail in Chapter Five, estimating the number of pregnancies is very difficult. The tables here bring together the best sources for each type of statistic. The year 1983 was chosen because it was the latest year for which both birth and abortion data are available, for women ages nineteen and below.

The number of pregnancies was calculated by adding together the number of births, abortions, and miscarriages. Of those three categories of data, the annual total of births is the most reliable. Births must be reported to a government agency, and they are complied into vital statistics. Federal reports of national totals are used here.

Unfortunately, abortion statistics are not collected in nearly as systematic a fashion. The tables here use the annual abortion totals published by Planned Parenthood's research arm, the Alan Guttmacher Institute, rather than the federal government's Center for Disease Control because the Institute's figures are generally acknowledged to be more accurate. Moreover, utilizing statistics provided by the nation's largest abortion promoter and provider of abortions avoids any problem with being accused of giving the data a pro-life slant. An analysis of the relative strengths and weaknesses of the collection methods of the Guttmacher Institute and the Centers for Disease Control is available in "Underreporting from States Invalidates New Federal Report On Number of Abortions" (Glasow 1987b, 11).

Establishing a definite figure for the annual total of miscarriages, the final component which must be added in to determine the annual total of pregnancies, is even more difficult. (Another name for miscarriage is spontaneous abortion, as distinct from induced abortion—the intentional killing of an unborn child.) There are no definite statistics for miscarriages for a variety of reasons, including the fact that women often do not report them. Estimates of the incidence of miscarriages vary widely. The tables here employ a method of estimating the annual number that was used in *Risking The Future*, a book which strongly endorsed school-based clinics (Hayes 1987). This method probably overestimates the annual number of miscarriages significantly, but again we use the method because it avoids any taint of swaying the results in a pro-life direction. The calculation of the number of miscarriages is described in the note for each table.

In sum, then, the following *estimates* for the number of pregnancies in 1983 was calculated by adding annual numbers of births, abortions, and miscarriages from the sources described above.

Pregnancies, Births, Abortions, and Miscarriages To Adolescents in 1983
(Latest year available)

Category	Statistics		Percent of total pregnancies
Abortions			
married	17,040		1.6
unmarried	410,640		38.4
total		427,680	40.0
Births			
married	228,962		21.4
unmarried	270,076		5.3
total		499,038	46.7
Miscarriages			
married	47,496		4.4
unmarried	95,079		8.9
total		142,575	13.3
Total Adolescent Pregnancies		**1,072,293**	**100.0**

Sources: Number of abortions: Stanley K. Henshaw, "Characteristics of U.S. Women Having Abortions, 1982-1983," *Family Planning Perspectives* v. 19, no. 1 (January/February, 1987), Table 4, p. 8. Number of births: National Center for Health Statistics, "Advance Report of Final Natality Statistics, 1983," *Monthly Vital Statistics Report*, v. 34, no. 6, Supplement, 1985, Table 17 (live births to unmarried women) and Table 2 (total number of live births by age group). Number of miscarriages: calculated as 20% of births plus 10% of abortions, according to a model developed by C. Tietze and J. Bongaarts of the Population Council, cited in 'Risking The Future', v. II, p. A64/416. Percentages calculated based on total pregnancies.

Pregnancies, Births, Abortions, and Miscarriages To Adolescents in 1983 By Marital Status
(Latest year available)

Category	Statistics		Percent of total pregnancies
Married			
abortions	17,040		1.6
births	228,962		21.4
miscarriages	47,496		4.4
total		293,498	27.4
Unmarried			
abortions	410,640		38.4
births	270,076		25.3
miscarriages	95,079		8.9
total		775,795	72.6
Total Adolescent Pregnancies		1,072,293	100.0

Sources: Number of abortions: Stanley K. Henshaw, "Characteristics of U.S. Women Having Abortions, 1982-1983," *Family Planning Perspectives* v. 19, no. 1 (January/February, 1987), Table 4, p. 8. Number of births: National Center for Health Statistics, "Advance Report of Final Natality Statistics, 1983," *Monthly Vital Statistics Report*, v. 34, no. 6, Supplement, 1985, Table 17 (live births to unmarried women) and Table 2 (total number of live births by age group). Number of miscarriages: calculated as 20% of births plus 10% of abortions, according to a model developed by C. Tietze and J. Bongaarts of the Population Council, cited in *Risking The Future*, v. II, p. A64/416. Percentages calculated based on total pregnancies.

Pregnancies, Births, Abortions, and Miscarriages To Married Adolescents in 1983
(Latest year available)

Category	Statistics	Percent of total pregnancies
Abortions	17,040	5.8
Births	228,962	78.0
Miscarriages	47,496	16.2
TOTAL	293,498	100.0

Sources: Number of abortions: Stanley K. Henshaw, "Characteristics of U.S. Women Having Abortions, 1982-1983," *Family Planning Perspectives* v. 19, no. 1 (January/February, 1987), Table 4, p. 8. Number of births: National Center for Health Statistics, "Advance Report of Final Natality Statistics, 1983," *Monthly Vital Statistics Report*, v. 34, no. 6, Supplement, 1985, Table 17 (live births to unmarried women) and Table 2 (total number of live births by age group). Number of miscarriages: calculated as 20% of births plus 10% of abortions, according to a model developed by C. Tietze and J. Bongaarts of the Population Council, cited in *Risking The Future*, v. II, p. A64/416. Percentages calculated based on total pregnancies to married adolescents.

Pregnancies, Births, Abortions, and Miscarriages To Unmarried Adolescents in 1983
(Latest year available)

Category	Statistics	Percent of total pregnancies
Abortions	410,640	52.9
Births	270,076	34.8
Miscarriages	95,079	12.3
TOTAL	775,795	100.0

Sources: Number of abortions: Stanley K. Henshaw, "Characteristics of U.S. Women Having Abortions, 1982-1983," *Family Planning Perspectives* v. 19, no. 1 (January/February, 1987), Table 4, p. 8. Number of births: National Center for Health Statistics, "Advance Report of Final Natality Statistics, 1983," *Monthly Vital Statistics Report*, v. 34, no. 6, Supplement, 1985, Table 17 (live births to unmarried women) and Table 2 (total number of live births by age group). Number of miscarriages: calculated as 20% of births plus 10% of abortions, according to a model developed by C. Tietze and J. Bongaarts of the Population Council, cited in *Risking The Future*, v. II, p. A64/416. Percentages calculated based on total pregnancies to unmarried adolescents.

APPENDIX TWO

Planned Parenthood Study on Teen Pregnancy Seriously Flawed and Misleading

An often-quoted article analyzing the problem of teenage pregnancy published in 1985 by Planned Parenthood's Alan Guttmacher Institute stimulated enormous media and public interest. Appearing in the March/April issue of *Family Planning Perspectives*, the article, titled "Teenage Pregnancy in Developed Countries: Determinants and Policy Implications," attempted to finger key social, economic, and political conditions in the United States that accounted for the escalating numbers of pregnancies to unmarried teenaged girls (Jones 1985, 53-63). It was later published in 1986 in book form by the same team of authors under the title of *Teenage Pregnancy in Industrialized Countries* (Jones 1986), and the comments here about the 1985 article apply equally to the book version.

Unfortunately, both government officials and the media almost uniformly accepted uncritically and virtually without reservation the Guttmacher Institute's assessment of the causes and solutions to the teen pregnancy "epidemic" without recognizing either the inherent biases of the authors or the serious methodological gaps and flaws in their research.

The crux of the Institute's article was a comparison between the United States, which has a relatively high incidence of teen pregnancy, and selected foreign countries which have lower teen pregnancy rates. It sought to answer two major questions: why U.S. rates were higher, and what could be learned from foreign countries that could be "useful for reducing the number of teenage conceptions in the United States" (Jones 1985, 53; page references listed are to *Family Planning Perspectives*.)

The team of eight authors failed to offer a definite answer to their first question: the causes of the comparatively higher pregnancy rates among U.S. teens, which is not surprising in light of the inadequacy of their research (Jones 1985, 60). Yet, despite having only vague information about the nature of the problem, the researchers forged ahead to offer a "solution."

Their article was hugely successful in framing the policy debate. Their identification of several different types of programs employed by the other countries which the article contends "improve the situation"—such as sex education and more widespread use of teen health clinics—was hailed as examples of the kind of actions that the United States should emulate.

The title of the article emphasizes that it is a multinational comparison of "pregnancy rates," but that is not actually the subject of the study. Casual readers may not have noticed that the Guttmacher Institute researchers decided to use statistics on birth rates instead of pregnancy rates, and the team of authors justified this major decision by assuming that birth rates could be an adequate substitute for pregnancy rates (Jones 1985, 53). While the researchers' assumption may seem reasonable, the data they presented should not be considered completely trustworthy, especially considering the source.

In view of these considerations, the conclusions drawn by the Guttmacher Institute researchers are open to serious challenge. Legislators, administrators, and the public should not rely on this flawed study. They should search for other sources of information to help assess the teenage pregnancy problem before they set goals and formulate specific plans.

The mainstream right-to-life movement, of course, takes no position on sex education, per se, except when it is used by Planned Parenthood and others to promote abortion. However, very serious concerns have arisen over the establishment of in-school health clinics and educational programs, which are being heavily promoted by abortion providers such as Planned Parenthood as a means to increase their accessibility to pregnant teenage girls.

Many pro-lifers realize that widespread adoption of the anti-life programs recommended by Guttmacher Institute, the Planned Parenthood Federation of America, and other groups would significantly increase the outreach of their pro-abortion educational efforts and encourage more teenagers to use their facilities which counsel, refer, and perform abortions. Thus it is very important to carefully scrutinize the research which pro-abortion organizations such as Guttmacher Institute offer to support their "solutions."

Absence of Crucial Data

One should immediately note the built-in bias of the authors, who are employees of organizations that would secure a huge share of millions of dollars in programs if the state and federal governments enacted the kind of proposals recommended in "Teen Pregnancy in Developed Countries." As explained in Chapter Three, the Guttmacher Institute receives a substantial portion of its income from PPFA, the nation's largest "reproductive health care" organization, which currently receives over 40% of its income from federal and state government sources.

One example of potential new sources of income is a new teen pregnancy initiative that almost passed the House of Representatives in 1985. It would have made available an additional $150 million dollars in its first two years. In light of this, it is probably not coincidental that the publication of the March 1985 article coincided with Planned Parenthood's renewed lobbying for reauthorization of Title X, its principal federal funding program, which provides money for abortion counseling and referrals.

Few legislators or members of the media have challenged Guttmacher Institute's lack of objectivity in proposing these new programs which would pour millions into its coffers. However, one could easily imagine the skepticism (if not outright hostility) that would greet the publication by a right-to-life organization of an article analyzing the hazards of induced abortion, especially if it was based on poor quality research.

Methodological Flaws in the Study

The fact that the Guttmacher Institute's researchers are not disinterested scholars, however, is not the major problem with this research project on teenage pregnancy. There are serious methodological shortcomings, some of which are acknowledged by the authors to exist in the data, and others which they omitted mentioning.

A brief description of the project's goals and general approach is essential to understanding the methodological flaws.

The study, funded by the Ford Foundation, sought to answer two questions. First, why were teenage pregnancy rates higher in the United States than in thirty-seven other economically well-developed countries? Second, what could be learned from the experience of other countries with lower teen pregnancy rates and employed to reduce teen pregnancies in the United States? (Jones 1985, 53).

To answer these questions, the researchers presented a two-tiered analysis. They compared 42 general social, economic, and political variables across 37 countries.

In addition to collecting statistical data, Guttmacher Institute attempted to quantify subjective variables such as "openness to sex" and "religiosity" of the people by collecting opinions from embassy personnel and family planning officials in each country. They then more closely scrutinized five countries (in addition to the United States) that met three criteria: first, a similarity to the United States in cultural background and economic development; second, the availability of reliable statistical information; and third, lower teen pregnancy rates.

Two Categories of Methodological Flaws

The first methodological flaw was evident on the first page of the *Perspectives* article. Readers of the Institute's study should have (but, one suspects, didn't) take very seriously the authors' caution that "[t]he *results* of the multivariate analysis [of data from 37 countries] presented here have to be taken as *suggestive rather than conclusive*, and they are described only in broad terms" (Jones 1985, 53; emphasis added). Indeed, a table of statistical data in the appendix to the article shows how weak their data was.

In 34% of the variables used in the study, less than half of the countries reported information. In many cases, only 13 or 14 countries were listed in the tables as a basis for making comparisons (Jones 1985, 62).

In addition, the inquisitive reader would find buried in the appendix two other illuminating caveats about the quality of the data. The authors admit that their analysis was hampered by missing data. Therefore, for example, they are unsure whether the "lack of correlation" between birthrates and the economic and social variable "indicates the absence of a relationship or is due to shortcomings in the data" (Jones 1985, 61).

Moreover, the Guttmacher Institute's researchers recognized that much of the data that they used in the 37-country study was subject to a *"considerable margin of error"* because it resulted from "informed observation rather than quantitative fact" (Jones 1985, 61; emphasis added). Rather than conducting authoritative public opinion surveys, they attempted (as mentioned above) to measure highly subjective factors such as "openness about sex" and the "religiosity" of each country by questioning embassy personnel or family planning officials.

Acknowledging Problems with the Six-Country Analysis

The researchers gave heavy emphasis to the six-country analysis of the United States, Canada, England and Wales, France, the Netherlands, and Sweden; they devoted over 60% of the article to it. Therefore, the methodological deficiencies in this important section further undercut any pretense that the study should be a definitive guide to policy.

Cross-cultural analysis such as that found in the article is inherently risky because of the large number of assumptions necessary to make any comparisons. Indeed, the Guttmacher Institute's researchers acknowledged the cultural, social, economic, and political differences between the United States and the other five countries in the study. Nevertheless, they went ahead and conducted the analysis anyway (Jones 1985, 58-61).

The validity of the six-country analysis appears highly questionable in light of the following seven major differences between the United States and the other nations.

- The other five countries have smaller populations.
- They are more compact geographically, except Canada which only has a smaller population.
- They are less heterogeneous racially, which is especially important in light of the high abortion rate among blacks in the United States.
- The research team found that religion had a "less pervasive" influence in the other five countries.
- Their governments were generally more centralized than the United States, which had important implications in policy decisions about abortion and related issues.
- Moreover, all five had instituted more wide-ranging social welfare systems, and income distribution was less unequal than in the United States.
- Finally, the right-to-life and pro-family movements, which have a major role in U.S. political affairs, are not as powerful and well-funded in the other five countries.

A Hidden Deficiency

The inability to present statistical data about teenage pregnancy rates is crucial because the article has been put forward as an analysis of "Teenage Pregnancy in Developed Countries." However, as mentioned above, the study is actually correlating birth rates—not pregnancy rates— with the other economic, social, and political factors. Therefore, birth rates (which do not account for abortions and miscarriages) and not pregnancy rates provided the baseline for all of the multi-national comparisons (Jones 1985, 53).

Conclusion

Since mid-1985, Planned Parenthood utilized its research arm, the Alan Guttmacher Institute, to capitalize on the growing public concern over the alarming rate of teenage pregnancy. Adroitly manipulating the media, the Institute used the publication of its multinational comparative study as a springboard for promoting massive increases in Planned Parenthood's government funding.

Anyone planning to use Guttmacher Institute's article should be made aware of the inherent biases of the researchers and the methodological flaws in their work. In the face of these glaring deficiencies, policymakers should be highly skeptical of the conclusions drawn in the study about the causes of teen pregnancy. Moreover, Guttmacher Institute's policy recommendations should be recognized as Planned Parenthood's self-serving attempt to win government funding for its pet programs.

Policymakers should look elsewhere for information about the teen pregnancy issue.

APPENDIX THREE

Outcome Evaluation and Process Evaluation of School-Based Clinics

T he book *Risking the Future,* written by National Research Council's panel studying adolescent pregnancy, provided a two-fold standard (or model) to use in evaluating the quality of the data about the influence of SBCs. In the chapter prescribing "priorities for future data collection and research," the NRC panel recommended wider and more effective use of both "outcome evaluation" and "process evaluation" (Hayes 1987, 250-251).

"Outcome Evaluation"

According to the experts, outcome evaluation is essential to assess "the effectiveness of an intervention strategy in achieving its specified objectives" (Hayes 1987, 250-251). Continues their report, "typically, outcome evaluation involves establishing 'before' and 'after' measures of program activity and comparing them to a control group that was not exposed to the program."

The NRC report cautioned that outcome evaluation required both the availability of a suitable program to study and an extensive commitment of resources in time, financial support and technical assistance. For these reasons, it can only be done on a limited basis.

A simple illustration of how outcome evaluation could be applied to SBCs might be helpful. Before opening the clinic, the research team would attempt to measure pregnancy rates and the abortion rates among teenagers in two comparable schools. Then the clinic would open and operate in one school, while the other school without the clinic would serve as the "control." After a suitable period of time, researchers would measure the pregnancy and abortion rates at both schools again. A statistical comparison of the pregnancy and abortion rates "before" and "after" the test period should indicate whether the clinic had any effect on the students' actions.

In this example, the validity of the evaluation strategy depends heavily on the method of collecting the data, on a consistent SBC program during the study period, and on having comparable student bodies in race, socio-economic composition, size, and similar factors.

"Process Evaluation"

The NRC panel also suggested wider use of "process evaluation" which has different and more short-range objectives. "Service providers [i.e., the SBC staff members] are often less interested," observed the NRC report, "in evaluation for its capability to measure outcomes than for its capability to provide information for program improvement" (Hayes 1987, 251). This observation aptly characterized the evaluation strategy of SBC staff and researchers. They focus on making modifications in the program "to improve its efficiency and responsiveness to the needs of the clients," stated the NRC report.

Process evaluation methods used in SBCs have included measuring clinic attendance, student attendance, and the services which are most in demand, and the usage of contraceptives (Kirby 1985, 13-14).

Putting the Methods to Use?

Ironically, the NRC panel failed to subject the "facts" from St. Paul and other clinics to rigorous scrutiny using the standards listed elsewhere in their book (Hayes 1987, 169-173). The panel acknowledged that SBCs had some limitations, but not surprisingly, *Risking the Future* endorsed SBCs as a "promising intervention for reducing early unintended pregnancy" for "implementation and evaluation for schools with large, high-risk populations" (Hayes 1987, 275).

ENDNOTES

Chapter One

What Is A "School-Based Clinic?"

1. In light of this disturbing development in school clinic staffing, it is not surprising that the National Association of School Nurses passed a resolution in June 1986 stating that they could support SBCs only if two conditions were met (Lordi 1987a, 7). First, the facilities must "supplement, not supplant, school nurses." And second, school nurses must "be integrally involved in the design, development, and implementation of SBCs and serve as the nursing professional in the SBC model."

2. Dr. John C. Willke, President of National Right to Life, has called attention to the fact that in most areas of the country, after the public becomes aware of the primary purpose of these in-school facilities, they are most commonly called "sex clinics" (Willke 1987).

Chapter Two

Promoting Abortion Referrals, Pro-Abortion Education, and Abortion Pills

1. This policy has been called the "sneak rule" because SBCs operate behind parents' backs.

2. The specific states were listed by the Center for Population Options in one of their publications in a table "States and Minor's Consent" (Center for Pop. Options 1986a, 3): "In 12 states where minors [definition varies] have the right to consent to their own medical care:" AL, AR, LA, MA, MI, MN, NV, NH, OH, RI, SC, WA.

    "Thirty-three states and the District of Columbia allow minors [definition varies] to consent to get contraceptives [and abortion counseling and referrals]:" AL, AK, AR, CA, CO, DE, DC, FL, GA, HI, ID, IL, KY, LA, ME, MA, MI, MN, MS, MT, NV, NH, NM, NY, NC, OH, OR, RI, SC, TN, TX, VA, and WA.

3. According to the booklet titled "School-Based Clinics: Update 1986" published in October 1986 by the Center for Population Options, Title X provided approximately 3% of the income for SBCs that year (Lovick and 1986, 13). Judging from that figure, SBCs are currently receiving only a fraction of the Title X national budget of over $130 million. This assessment is also consistent with a survey in 1986 conducted by the U.S. General Accounting Office (United States GAO 1986). Only one of the eighteen SBCs that responded to the questionnaire received Title X funds.

4. Kenney's statement regarding Title X requirements is unfortunately consistent with the current interpretation of the federal guidelines. However, on September 1, 1987 the federal Department of Health and Human Services proposed amending the regulations to return the Title X program to its original purpose of promoting family planning, not abortion (U.S. Dept. of Health and Human Services 1987). These changes implemented an order on July 30, 1987 from President Reagan to Dr. Otis Bowen, Secretary of Health and Human Services, "to ensure that no Title X funds to go any program that encourages, promotes or advocates abortion, or which assists a women in obtaining an abortion" (Associated Press 1987, A3). Right-to-life supporters have long maintained that the actual wording of the Title X legislation passed in 1970 did not require Title X grantees to provide abortion counseling and referrals, and in fact the statute and legislative history require a complete separation of the Title X services from any abortion-related activities, such as operating an abortion mill (Rich 1987). Pro-abortion advocates strongly support the status quo and recognize that this battle could have important ramifications on the policies in SBCs. They have threatened court action to block implementation of the proposed Title X changes, which they denounce vehemently (Greenhouse 1987, 8).

Chapter Three

Pro-Abortion Agenda of Clinic Promoters

1. News reports often provide Laurie S. Zabin with additional credibility as a commentator about the medical needs of teenagers by identifying her as a "doctor." However, they fail to note that she is not a physician (a M.D.), but a demographer (a Ph.D.) employed by the Johns Hopkins School of Hygiene and Public Health (Brozan 1986, C3; Henderson 1987).

Chapter Five

Misleading Claims About Reducing Pregnancies

1. A more recent analysis of the data from St. Paul published in December 1986 by the National Research Council's panel studying adolescent pregnancy reached the same conclusion. Without statistical data about "the trend in pregnancies and abortions," the NRC report pointed out, "we don't know how much of the decline in births is due to a decrease in pregnancies and how much to an increase in abortion" (Hayes 1987, 170).

Chapter Six

Undercutting Parental Authority

1. In 1983, the federal government attempted to restore a measure of parent-child communication by returning to a policy of notifying parents when a family planning clinic funded by federal Title X ("Title Ten" of the Public Health Service Act) gave medically hazardous drugs or devices to their minor child. The pro-abortion forces, supported by the media, vigorously opposed this policy, and they scored a public relations coup by dubbing it the "squeal rule." The right-to-life movement was not involved in this because it related to contraception and not to induced abortion.

    However, as Dr. John C. Willke, president of National Right to Life, has pointed out, the pro-abortion lobby has recently applied the label "squeal rule" with increasing frequency in the school-based clinic debate. The SBC proponents maintain that the clinics will be using a "squeal rule" if they breach the "confidentiality" of "reproductive health treatment" for minors by telling their parents about the treatment in the school-clinics (Willke 1987).

    Since the label apparently swayed public opinion once before, Dr. Willke and others in the pro-life movement are concerned that it would do so again. He proposed a set of counter semantics to neutralize the effect of the term "squeal rule" in public debates and media. His retort has been that when the clinics maintain "confidentiality," the staff is really using a "sneak rule"—that is, to help the students sneak behind their parents backs.

2. As the Center for Population Option's "SBC Update: 1986" revealed, several different types of organizations operate the best known SBCs: the

St. Paul-Ramsey Medical Center; a community clinic (Jackson-Hinds in Jackson, Mississippi); a private non-profit corporation under contract from a department of public health (DuSable in south Chicago); a private non-profit organization (Kansas City and Houston); a family planning clinic (Planned Parenthood in Muskegon, Michigan); and a school system (Gary, Indiana) (Lovick and Wesson 1986, 15-17).

3. SBC operators have demonstrated great ingenuity and flexibility in locating a wide variety of federal, state and local public and private monies. The Center for Population Options' survey in the summer of 1986 revealed that public funds contributed 64% of income and private sources 36% (Lovick and Wesson 1986, 13). State governments contributed 16%, community health gave 2%, and five separate federal sources provided a total of 46%—for a grand total of 64%. Of the 36% given from private sources, private foundations contributed most of it—31%. Private corporations and non-profit organizations gave a total of 3%, and patient fees, third-party reimbursements, and miscellaneous sources gave another 2%.

Chapter Eight

Local Coalitions Stopping Clinic Proposals

1. The experience in Washington, D.C. illustrates both the effect of careful behind-the-scenes lobbying and planning by clinic advocates and the impact of community-based opposition. Sharon Robinson, a consultant to Planned Parenthood of Washington, D.C. provided a detailed review of the events during a workshop on SBCs on March 6, 1986 at the annual meeting of the National Family Planning and Reproductive Health Association.

During 1984 and 1985, she said, a working group consisting of Planned Parenthood of Washington, D.C. (PPWDC) and city government officials in the mayor's office, school system, and health department worked out almost all the details for opening a clinic prior to any attempt to get community input. In December 1985, however, when the school board held the first meeting to solicit parental and community reaction to the proposal to open a clinic in the school that PPWDC and the city bureaucrats had chosen, the parents and religious leaders strongly objected. Faced with such opposition, Robinson and the other backers of the clinic retrenched (Robinson 1986).

But, the SBC program reemerged with only superficial changes in March 1987 (Dowling 1987, 10C). The health department had replaced PP of WDC as the operator, which removed one of the lightning rods for opposition. However, the general health program, including abortion counselling and referrals and illusory parental consent requirements, remains intact. The final outcome of the debate over the clinic remains to be seen.

2. Dryfoos' observation is not an isolated case. For example: "'They're well-meaning, concerned people with tunnel vision.' says [Mart] Hennrich [Roosevelt High School clinic coordinator] of the protestors" (Kantrowitz 1987, 57). U.S. Rep. Henry Waxman introduced a bill to pour $50 million into SBCs, and stated that "those who would oppose this legislation on the grounds that it promotes or encourages teenage sexuality, are, in effect, imposing their own moral judgements on every community in this country" (Center for Pop. Options 1986b, 2).

Chapter Nine

An Uncertain Future for SBCs

1. Selection from speech by Douglas Kirby, Ph.D., Director of Research of the Center for Population Options, Washington, D.C. on the "Effectiveness of School-Based Clinics" at the Sixteenth Annual Meeting of the National Family Planning and Reproductive Health Association, March 2, 1988, in Washington, D.C., session on "Education."

". . . At the Center for Population Options, we have been engaging in a research project for several years on the impact of school-based clinics, and it really is on that research that I am going to report today.

"These findings that I report today are not final. We are collecting our last data tomorrow in East St. Louis [Illinois]. They are preliminary; but nevertheless, we do have enough data that I am reasonably confident that what I am going to say will hold true. A final report will be available [in] probably late summer or very early fall.

　　　. . .

"We find basically that there are no measurable—I want to under-line that word and put it in boldface—there is no measurable impact upon the use of birth control, nor *upon pregnancy rates* or birth rates. This is all based upon the survey data. *There is no measurable impact* (emphasis added)."

Audio tape recording and transcription by Richard D. Glasow.

REFERENCES USED

Note: Some audio tape recordings and non-trade publications used as references in this book were purchased or obtained from sources that may be difficult to locate. Those items are marked with an asterisk (*) and the addresses of the companies or agencies where they were purchased are provided at the end of this list.

Ahartz, Joanne, et al..
    1986. * *The St. Paul Story: A Working Manual On The Pioneer School-Based Clinics in St. Paul, Minnesota.* St. Paul: Health Start, Inc.

Alan Guttmacher Institute.
    1976.   *Annual Report.*

    1985.   *Annual Report.*

    1986.   "School-Based Health Program Helps Inner-City Teens Delay Sex and Prevent Pregnancy." Press Release. July 9.

Allegar, Bill.
    1985.   "50 Attend hearing on school clinic." *Washington Times,* December 12.

American Academy of Pediatrics.
    1987.   "AAP Guidelines: School-based Health Clinics." *AAP News,* 3:4.

Archdiocese of Boston. Family Life Office.
    1987. * "Report on School-Based Health Clinics." Boston: Daughters of St. Paul.

Archibald, George.
    1987.   "Bowen Testimony Defies Reagan On Abortion." *Washington Times,* February 19.

Associated Press.
    1986.   "Chicago School Clinic Is Sued." *New York Times,* October 16.

    1987.   "Reagan Would Bar Funds For Abortion Counseling." *Washington Post,* July 31.

Banas, Casey.
1986.   "Birth control set for 2d city school." *Chicago Tribune,* August 7.

Baulieu, Etienne-Emile.
1985.   "RU 486: An Antiprogestin Steroid With Contragestive Activity in Women." In *The Antiprogestin Steroid RU 486 and Human Fertility Control,* edited by Etienne-Emile Baulieu and Sheldon J. Segal. New York: Plenum Press.

Belka, John.
1986.   "A Step Too Far." Speech at workshop on "Portland Public Teen Sex Clinic." Right to Life of Oregon Annual Convention, October 25, in Portland, Oregon.

Bennett, David A. and Wanda Miller.
1986.   "School Clinics Help Curb Teen Pregnancy and Dropout Rate." *The School Administrator* (September).

Bennett, William J.
1986.   "Speech at Annual Meeting of Education Writers Assn." April 11, in Baltimore, Maryland. Transcript.

Berger, Ellis.
1986.   "Florida bishops oppose plan for ten sex-health clinics." *Miami [Florida] News,* April 24.

Berger, Leslie.
1986.   "Paterson clinic plan rejected; infighting blamed." *[Hackensack, New Jersey] Record,* December 19.

Bernstein, Leonard.
1986.   "Bishop's Stance Against School Clinic to Hit Pulpit." *Los Angeles Times,* April 12.

Brandon, Craig.
1986.   "School board OKs teen pregnancy study." *[Utica, New York] Observor-Dispatch,* December 17.

Brody, Jane E.
1986.   "Abortion Pill Expected to be Sold in Europe." *New York Times,* December 18.

Brozan, Nadine.
    1986.   "School Project Cuts Pregnancy Rates." *New York Times*, July
             10.

Callen, Kate.
    1986.   "'All-out war' mounted on teenage pregnancy." *[Monticello,
             Indiana] Herald Journal*, August 20.

Carnegie Corporation of New York.
    1985.   *Annual Report.*

Carreau, Mark.
    1986.   "Pregnancies create trap for teens." *Houston Chronicle*, Feb-
             ruary 23.

Carter, Judy.
    1985.   Ounce of Prevention Fund press release (not dated), distributed
             during workshop on "Media Techniques." National School-
             Based Clinic conference, October 6, 1986 in Denver, Colorado.

    1986.   Speech presented at workshop on "Media Techniques." Nation-
             al School-Based Clinic conference, October 6, in Denver, Colo-
             rado. (Audio tape recording by Richard D. Glasow—not for
             sale.)

Cathey, Anne.
    1987.   "School-Based Teen Health Centers in Multnomah County,
             Oregon." Testimony in U.S. Congress. House. 1987c.

Center for Population Options.
    1983.   "Statement of Judith Senderowitz, Executive Director." Press
             release, January 21.

    1985.   *Annual Report for the year ended March 31, 1985.*

    1986a.   "Parental Involvement." *Clinic News* 2 (3):5 (October).

    1986b.   "$50 Million School-Based Clinic Bill Introduced in Congress."
             Clinic News 2 (3):1 (October).

    1986c.   "City Task Forces Surveyed." *Issues & Action Update* 5 (1): 4-5
             (Winter).

    1986d. * *School-Based Clinic Policy Initiatives Around the Country:
             1985.*

1986e.   Workshop on "Parents: Consent and Confidentiality." National School-Based Clinic conference, October 7, in Denver, Colorado. (Audio tape recording by Richard D. Glasow—not for sale.)

1987a.   *Annual Report for the year ended March 31, 1987.*

1987b.   "Second Round of Robert Wood Johnson Grantees Announced." *Clinic News*, 3 (3):1 (October).

1987c.   "Around the Country. In the States." *Clinic News*, 3 (3):1 (October).

Children's Defense Fund.
1979.   *Annual Report.*

1987a.   "Adolescent Pregnancy: An Anatomy of a Social Problem in Search of Comprehensive Solutions."

1987b.   "An Overview of CDF's Print Campaign." (Handout at national annual meeting in Washington, D.C.)

Clardy, Jim.
1987.   "Clinic proposal jams first hearing." *Washington Times*. November 18.

Cole, Jeff.
1986.   "High school health clinic is approved." *Milwaukee Sentinel,* October 30.

Comer, James P.
1986.   "The Link Between Schools and Health." Speech presented at plenary session. National School-Based Clinic conference, October 7, in Denver, Colorado. (Audio tape recording by Richard D. Glasow—not for sale.)

Conley, Kim T.
1987.   "Vote defeats health clinic." *[Meriden, Connecticut] Record-Journal,* December 2.

Cook, Kevin.
1986.   "Planner of teen birth control clinics shrugs off torrent of criticism." *Washington Times,* May 2.

Cook, Lou.
    1986.   Letter to Editor. *Washington Post*, April 27.
    1987.   "This proposed health clinic triggered a rhetorical meltdown."
                 American School Board Journal (May).

Coughlan, Christopher.
    1987a. *   Speech at workshop on "School-Based Clinics: Ways to Counter—
                 State and Local." National Right to Life annual convention,
                 June 18, in New Orleans, Louisiana. (Audio cassette recording
                 of conference tape number 13 purchased from Cincinnati Right
                 to Life.)
    1987b.   "Males Preventing Pregnancy Conference—A Pro-Life Cri-
                 tique." (Quoting Joy Dryfoos' speech presented at Conference
                 on Male Involvement: A Strategy for Preventing Teen-Age
                 Pregnancy, June 11, at University of Maine, Orono, Maine.)

Crawford, Rev. Hiram v. Board of Education of the City of Chicago.
    1986.   Complaint for a preliminary and permanent injunction and
                 other relief. Circuit Court of Cook County, Illinois. Case
                 Number 86 CH 9829. Filed October 15.

Crockett, Kimberly and Sandy Theis.
    1986.   "Abortion foes fight teen clinics." *Cincinnati Inquirer*, August
                 27.

Curry, George. E.
    1986.   "U.S. teens 'swept away' by sex." *Chicago Tribune*, December
                 17.

Demsko, Tobin.
    1987.   "School-Based Health Clinics: An Analysis of the Johns Hop-
                 kins Study." *Research Developments*. Family Research Council,
                 March 26.

Dickey, Jim.
    1986.   "School clinics aren't just for controversy." *San Jose Mercury
                 News*, October 22.

Dine, Philip.
    1987.   "Missouri Balks at New Clinics for Schools." *St. Louis Post-
                 Dispatch*, August 25.

Dobson, James.
    1986.   "School-Based Health Clinics." Focus on the Family radio program, October 14 and 15.

Dolan, Cindy.
    1987.   "Health Panel To Withdraw School Plan." *Mexico [Missouri] Ledger*, February 18.

Doss, Rod.
    1986.   "Semantics Aside...Black Community Target of 'Sex Clinics'." *New Pittsburgh Courier*. Editorial, May 17.

Dowling, Carrie.
    1987.   "D.C. Panel approves policy for school health clinics." *Washington Times*, March 6.

Dryfoos, Joy.
    1985a.   "A Time for New Thinking about Teenage Pregnancy." *Amer. Jour. of Public Health* 75 (1):13-14 (January).

    1985b.   "School-Based Health Clinics." *Family Planning Perspectives* 17 (2):70-75 (March/April).

    1986a.   "Preventing Teen Pregnancy: What Works." *Planned Parenthood Review* 6 (2):6-7 (Spring).

    1986b. * "Research: 'What We Know'." In Scientists' Institute for Public Information, 1986.

    1986c.   "Update on School-Based Clinics: Fad or Social Movement." Speech presented at the National School-Based Clinic conference, October 6, in Denver, Colorado. (Audio tape recording by Richard D. Glasow—not for sale.)

Edwards, Laura F. et al.
    1980.   "Adolescent Pregnancy Prevention Services in High School Clinics." *Family Planning Perspectives*. 12 (1):6-7, 11-14 (January/February).

Fallon, Michael.
    1986.   "Funding for controversial health clinic denied." *Sacramento Union*, December 12.

Fisher, Marc.
1987.   "Confronting Teen-Age Sexuality." *Washington Post*, April 14.

Fitzgerald, Susan.
1986.   "School-based clinic for pregnant teens urged." *Philadelphia Inquirer*, March 27.

Flanery, James Allen.
1986.   "Attitude Shift Credited for Fall in Teen Births." *Omaha World-Herald*, March 2.

Foundation Center.
1985.   *Foundation Grants Index*. 14th ed.. New York.

1986a.   *Foundation Grants Index*. 15th ed.. New York.

1986b.   *Foundation Grants Bimonthly Index* (March-April).

1986c.   *Foundation Grants Bimonthly Index* (November-December).

1986d.   *COMSEARCH Printout: Abortion, Birth Control & Family Planning, 1986.*

1987a.   *Foundation Grants Bimonthly Index*. (January/February).

1987b.   *Foundation Grants Bimonthly Index*. (March/April).

1987c.   *Foundation Grants Bimonthly Index*. (May/June).

Foundation News.
1987.   "Of All Things." 28 (6):13 (November/December).

Franklin, James L.
1986.   "New pill may alter abortion debate." *Boston Globe*, December 22.

Franz, Wanda.
1986.   "Pro-Abortion Researchers Warn that Young People Increasingly Pro-Life." *National Right to Life News*, September 25.

Furstenberg, Frank F., Jr., Richard Lincoln, and Jane Menken, eds.
1981.   *Teenage Sexuality, Pregnancy, and Childbearing*. Philadelphia: University of Philadelphia Press.

Gasper, Jo Ann.
1986.   "Adolescent Pregnancy and Childbearing." Written statement

before a hearing of the Joint Subcommittee Studying Teenage
Pregnancy of the Virginia Legislature, September 5, in Alexandria, Virginia.

Gauntt, Tom.
  1986.   "Roosevelt clinic continues to breed controversy." *St. Johns
              [Oregon] Review*, March 27.

Glasow, Richard D.
  1986.   "Abortionists Yank School-based Clinic Bill After Pro-Lifers
              Amend Proposal to Exclude Abortion and Abortion Provid-
              ers." *National Right to Life News*, April 10.

  1987a.   "Survey Confirms That Planned Parenthood Is Largest Abor-
              tion Provider in United States." *National Right to Life News*,
              December 3.

  1987b.   "Underreporting from States Invalidates New Federal Report
              On Number of Abortions." *National Right to Life News*, Sep-
              tember 10.

Greenhouse, Linda.
  1987.   "Reagan and Abortion. Restrictions on Money for Counseling
              Appear Vulnerable to Legal Challenge." *New York Times*,
              August 1.

Gribben, Anne M.
  1986.   Testimony before a hearing of the Joint Subcommittee Studying
              Teenage Pregnancy of the Virginia Legislature. September 5, in
              Alexandria, Virginia.

Gurule, David.
  1987. *   Speech presented at workshop on "Comprehensive Adolescent
              Health Services: Advocacy Strategies." National conference of
              the Children's Defense Fund, March 13, in Washington, D.C..
              (Audio cassette recording of conference tape number 22 pur-
              chased from Visual Aids Electronics.)

Hadley, Elaine M., Sharon R. Lovick, and Douglas Kirby.
  1986. *   *School-Based Health Clinics: A Guide to Implementing Pro-
              grams.* Washington, D.C.: Center for Population Options.

Haffner, Debra.
   1986.   *   Speech presented at workshop on "Adolescent Health Clinics:
               Services for an At-Risk Population." National conference of the
               Children's Defense Fund, February 28, in Washington, D.C.
               (Audio cassette recording of conference tape number 13 pur-
               chased from Visual Aids Electronics Corp.)

Harris, Louis and Associates.
   1985.   *Public Attitudes About Sex Education, Family Planning, and
            Abortion in the United States.* Poll conducted for the Planned
            Parenthood Federation of America. Study No. 854005, field-
            work August-September, 1985.

   1986.   *American Teens Speak: Sex, Myths, TV and Birth Control.* Poll
            conducted for the Planned Parenthood Federation of America,
            Project 864012, fieldwork September-October, 1986.

Hayes, Cheryl D., ed.
   1987.   *   *Risking The Future. Adolescent Sexuality, Pregnancy, and
               Childbearing.* Vol. I. National Research Council, Panel on Ado-
               lescent Pregnancy and Childbearing. Washington, D.C.: Nation-
               al Academy Press.

Henderson, Randi.
   1987.   "Fighting teen pregnancy: Laurie Schwab Zabin takes on one of
            the city's toughest problems." *The [Baltimore] Sun,* January 18.

Henshaw, Stanley K.
   1987.   "Characteristics of U.S. Women Having Abortions, 1982-
            1983." *Family Planning Perspectives* 19 (1):5-8 (January/
            February).

Henshaw, Stanley K., Jacqueline D. Forrest, and Jennifer Van Vort.
   1987.   "Abortion Services in the United States, 1984 and 1985." *Fam-
            ily Planning Perspectives* 19 (2):63-70 (March/April).

Herceg-Baron, Roberta et al.
   1986.   "Supporting Teenagers' Use of Contraceptives: A Comparison
            of Clinic Services." *Family Planning Perspectives* 18 (2): 61-66
            (March/April).

Hernandez, Peggy.
   1987.   "Clinic effort crystallizes potential schools advocacy group."
             Boston Globe, January 12.

Hewlett Foundation.
   1985.   *Annual Report.*

Hicks, Nancy.
   1969.   "Egeberg Proposes Drive to Promote Smaller Families." *New
             York Times*, October 31.

Hicks, Toni, et al.
   1986.   "San Diego Unified School District Task Force on School-
             Based Health Clinics. Minority Report." July 1.

Hoffreth, Sandra L. and Cheryl D. Hayes, ed.
   1987.   * *Risking The Future. Adolescent Sexuality, Pregnancy, and
             Childbearing*. Vol. II. Working Papers and Statistical Appen-
             dices. National Research Council, Panel on Adolescent Preg-
             nancy and Childbearing. Washington, D.C.: National Academy
             Press.

Holt, Cleve.
   1986.   Comment made from the audience during workshop on "Par-
             ents: Consent and Confidentiality." National School-Based
             Clinic conference. October 7, in Denver, Colorado. (Audio tape
             recording by Richard D. Glasow—not for sale.)

Horan, Dennis J., Edward R. Grant, and Paige C. Cunningham.
   1987.   *Abortion and the Constitution*. Washington, D.C.: Georgetown
             University Press. "Appendix One, Supreme Court Decisions on
             Abortion since 1973: A Summary."

Hurlbutt, Edward.
   1987.   * Speech at workshop on "School-Based Clinics: Ways to Counter—
             State and Local." National Right to Life annual convention,
             June 18, in New Orleans, Louisiana. (Audio cassette recording
             of conference tape number 8 purchased from Cincinnati Right
             to Life.)

Hurley, Dan.
   1986.   "From School Clinics, First-Line Health Care." *New York Times*, November 26.

Jacob, John E.
   1987.   "School Clinics Can Help Teen Pregnancy Problem." *Clinic News* 2 (4):6 (January).

James, Kay.
   1987.   "School-Based Clinics. Should we have them in public schools? No Thanks." Congressional Black Caucus. *Point of View* 25-26 (Summer).

Johnson, Douglas.
   1986.   "New Battle Looms Over U.S. Aid for U.N. Agency Supporting Coerced Abortion." *National Right to Life News*, May 1.

Jones, Elise F., et al.
   1985.   "Teenage Pregnancy in Developed Countries: Determinants and Policy Implications." *Family Planning Perspectives* 17 (2):53-63 (March/April).

   1986.   *Teenage Pregnancy in Industrialized Countries*. A Study Sponsored by the Alan Guttmacher Institute. New Haven: Yale University Press.

Kaegi, Louise.
   1985.   "School-Based Health Clinics: A Formidable New Twist in the Teen Sexuality Debate." *Family Protection Report* 8 (11):1-5 (November).

   1987.   Personal Communication.

Kantrowitz, Barbara.
   1987.   "Kids and Contraceptives." *Newsweek*, February 16.

Kapp, Lucy.
   1986.   "The Health Educator." In Ahartz, 1986.

Kasun, Jacqueline R.
   1986.   "The Baltimore School Birth Control Study: A Comment." Unpublished. Humboldt University, Arcata, California.

Katz, Gregory.
    1986.   "Sex clinics for teens ignite uproar." *USA Today*, November 11.

Kaye, Tony.
    1986.   "Are You for RU 486?" *New Republic* (January 27).

Keenan, Terrance.
    1985.   "The Governance of School-Based Adolescent Health Centers."
             (The Center for Population Options.) *Clinic News* 1 (2):6-7
             (April).

Kenney, Asta.
    1986a.   "School-Based Clinics: A National Conference." *Family Plan-
             ning Perspectives* 18 (1):44-46 (January/February).

    1986b.   Speech presented at workshop on "Parents: Consent and Confi-
             dentiality." National School-Based Clinic conference, October
             7, in Denver, Colorado. (Audio tape recording by Richard D.
             Glasow—not for sale.)

Kirby, Douglas.
    1985. * *School-Based Clinics: An Emerging Approach to Improving
             Adolescent Health and Addressing Teenage Pregnancy.* Wash-
             ington, D.C.: Center for Population Options.

    1986.   Speech presented at plenary session on "Research Update."
             National School-Based Clinic conference, October 7, in Denver,
             Colorado. (Audio tape recording by Richard D. Glasow—not
             for sale.)

Kissling, Frances and Judith Senderowitz.
    1986.   Letter from Catholics for a Free Choice endorsing Center for Pop-
             ulation Options' Adolescents and Abortion Survey. August 7.

Kitzi, Gerald.
    1986.   "Measuring the Behavorial Effects of a SBCs." Speech at plen-
             ary session on "Research Update." National School-Based Clinic
             conference, October 7, in Denver, Colorado. (Audio tape record-
             ing by Richard D. Glasow—not for sale.)

Knox, Richard A.
    1986.   "Abortion pill tests show it 85% effective." *Boston Globe*,
             December 18.

Kollars, Deb.
   1986.   "Emotions fly over health units." *Sacramento Bee*, September
             16.

Langmyhr, George.
   1971.   "The Role of Planned Parenthood-World Population in Abor-
             tion." *Clin. Obstet. Gynec.* 14.

Lardner, Joyce.
   1986.   "Birth Control Clinics in the Schools?" *Washington Post*, com-
             mentary, April 27.

Leo, John.
   1986.   "Sex and Schools." *TIME* (November 24).

Levin-Epstein, Jodie.
   1986a. * Speech presented at workshop on "School-Based Family Plan-
             ning Clinics." Annual meeting of the National Family Planning
             and Reproductive Health Assn., March 6, in Washington, D.C.
             (Audio cassette recording of conference tape number 8 pur-
             chased from Castle Sound and Video.)

   1986b.   Speech presented at workshop on "Parents: Consent and Confi-
             dentiality." National School-Based Clinic conference, October
             7, in Denver, Colorado. (Audio tape recording by Richard D.
             Glasow—not for sale.)

Lindquist, Diane and Christopher Reynolds.
   1986.   "Bishop's letter opposes school health clinics." *San Diego
             Union*, April 5.

Lordi, Sharon.
   1987a.   "Introduction to School-Based Clinics." (National Assn. of
             School Nurses.) *School Nurse* 7 (March/April).

   1987b.   "Starting Up." (National Assn. of School Nurses.) *School Nurse*
             24-27 (March/April).

   1987c.   "What the Future Holds." (National Assn. of School Nurses.)
             School Nurse 36-38 (March/April).

Lovick, Sharon R.
   1986.   "SBCs: The Future." Speech presented at plenary session.

National School-Based Clinic conference, October 7, in Denver, Colorado. (Audio tape recording by Richard D. Glasow—not for sale.)

1987a. *   Speech presented at workshop on "Comprehensive Adolescent Health Advocacy Strategies." National conference of the Children's Defense Fund, March 13, in Washington, D.C. (Audio cassette recording of conference tape number 22 purchased from Visual Aids Electronics.)

1987b.   Speech presented at plenary session on "Building Community Consensus in the Face of Opposition." National School-Based Clinic Conference, November 6, in Kansas City, Missouri. (Audio tape recording by Richard D. Glasow—not for sale.)

1987c. *   "The School-Based Clinic Update 1987." Washington, D.C: Center for Population Options.

Lovick, Sharon R. and Wanda F. Wesson.
1986.   *   "School-Based Clinic: Update 1986." Washington, D.C.: Center for Population Options.

McGrath, Mary.
1987.   "School health clinic again at issue." *Sacramento Union*, April 28.

McNamara, Connie.
1986.   "Family planner urges school-based birth control clinics." *Harrisburg [PA] News*, December 17.

MacNeil/Lehrer Newshour.
1986.   Focus Segment, "Birth Control Battle." November 24.

Madison, Nathaniel.
1986.   "School clinics in doubt." *Dayton News*, October 18.

Mathews, Jay.
1985.   "School Health-Clinic Movement Is Spreading Across the Nation." *Washington Post*, December 7.

Moran, Alfred.
1984.   *   Remarks at workshop on "Analysis of 1984 Elections: State and Federal." Annual meeting of the National Abortion Federa-

tion, May 16, in Los Angeles, California. (Audio cassette recording of conference tape number 18 purchased from American Audio Association.)

Moreland, Pamela.
1987.   "School Clinic Foes Target Charitable Foundation." *Los Angeles Times* (valley edition), June 1.

Morrissey James M., Adele M. Hofmann, and Jeffrey C. Thrope
1986.   *Consent and Confidentiality in the Health Care of Children and Adolescents: A Legal Guide.* New York: The Free Press.

Muskegon Area Planned Parenthood.
1985a.   "Summary. Muskegon Heights School-Based Teen Clinic."

1985b.   "Muskegon Heights Middle School Teen Health Center Evaluation, Second School Year Report, September 1984-June 1985."

New York City, Human Resources Administration.
1986.   "Research Summary: School-Based Health Clinics and Teenage Pregnancy," RS#86-1, June.

Ob. Gyn. News.
1987.   "Teen Polls Shows Confidentiality, Cost Key Issues in Contraception" (February 1-14).

O'Brien, Joan.
1987.   "Ensure Access to Abortions, Speaker Says." *Salt Lake City Tribune*, May 19.

O'Connor, Phillip. J.
1985.   "Pill Goes To School." *Chicago Sun-Times*, September 15.

Origins.
1987.   "Statement on School-Based Clinics." (NC Documentary Service.) 17 (25):432-441 (December 3).

Overman, Stephenie.
1987.   "Bishops Call for Amended School Board Policies." (National Catholic News Service.) *Arlington [Virginia] Catholic Herald*, November 17.

1985.   Factsheet. 3 pages.

1986.   "Comprehensive School-Based Health Clinics Profile," pamphlet.

Patton, Joan.
1986a.   "The California Alliance Concerned with School Age Parents (CACSAP). Highlights of Two Workshops on School-Based Clinics. November 13, 14, 15. San Diego, California." Tape transcription of speech by Kathleen Arnold-Sheeran.

1986b.   "Newsletter," Coalition for Family Values, August 27, quoting John Witt, San Diego school board member.

Perkes, Kim Sue.
1987.   "Teen Pregnancy Rates Keep Rising." *[Scottsdale, Arizona] Daily Progress*, January 2.

Perlez, Jane.
1986a.   "Educator Is Critical of Sex Policy in Schools." *New York Times*, October 9.

1986b.   "In New York, Storm Over Contraceptives in School." *New York Times*, October 12.

1986c.   "School Board Adopts New Consent Form." *New York Times*, November 20.

1986d.   "Schools Backed On Birth Curbs." *New York Times*, October 7.

1986e.   "Sex a Health Issue at New York School Clinics." *New York Times*, October 15.

1986f.   "Wagner to Seek School Contraceptives Limit." *New York Times*, October 8.

1986g.   "9 New York High Schools Dispense Contraceptives to Their Students." *New York Times*, October 6.

Pierce, Neal.
1986.   "St. Paul's Way of Forestalling Teen Pregnancies." *The [Baltimore] Sun*, February 24.

Pilpel, Harriet.
1983.   "Remarks of Harriet Pilpel, Esq. at 10th Anniversary *Roe v. Wade* — Pro-Choice Press Conference." January 21.

Planned Parenthood Federation of America.
1975. *A Five-Year Plan: 1976-1980. October 22.*

1983. *Annual Report—Charitable Organization, year ended 12-31-83. Enclosure, Form 990, Part I, Line 16, Schedule. Files of New York Department of State.*

1986a. *Making Possible the Promise of Adolescence. Service Report for 1985.*

1986b. "Planned Parenthood Programs to Combat Teen Pregnancy." *Planned Parenthood Review.* 6 (2):17-36 (Spring).

1987a. *Celebrating 70 Years of Service. 1986 Annual Report.*

1987b. *Service Report for 1986.*

Prater, Constance.
1987. "Teen Clinic Squelched by Parents in Taylor." *The Detroit News*, October 29.

Purser, Steve.
1986. * Speech presented at workshop on "School-Based Family Planning Clinics". Annual meeting of the National Family Planning and Reproductive Health Assn., March 6, in Washington, D.C. (Audio cassette recording of conference tape number 8 purchased from Castle Sound and Video.)

Raspberry, William.
1986. "Birth Control Clinics in Schools? No." *Washington Post*, April 14.

Regan, Elizabeth.
1986. "Prevention: Teen pregnancy battle begins." *Norfolk Virginian Pilot*, February 21.

Reynolds, Christopher.
1986. "School board drops plan for health clinic." *San Diego Union*, July 9.

Rich, Spencer.
1987. "Family Planning Program Faces Funding Battle." *Washington Post*, July 29.

Richburg, Keith B.
    1986.   "Bennett Criticizes Birth-Control Clinics." *Washington Post*,
               April 12.

Rifkin, Ira.
    1986.   "School Clinics Assailed." *[Los Angeles] Daily News* (valley
               edition), November 7.

Right to Life Education Foundation.
    1986.   "Sex Clinics Voted Down." Cincinnati. (November).

Robert Wood Johnson Foundation.
    1985.   "Special Report, National School Health Services Program."
               No. 1.

    1986a.   "Guidelines for Grant Applications to the School-Based Ado-
               lescent Health Care Program." With letter from Philip J. Porter,
               M.D., Director, July 17.

    1986b.   "School-Based Adolescent Health Care Program." April.

Robinson, Sharon.
    1986.   Speech at workshop on "School Based Family Planning Clin-
               ics." Annual meeting of the National Family Planning and
               Reproductive Health Assn., March 6, in Washington, D.C..
               (Audio cassette recording of conference tape number 8 pur-
               chased from Castle Sound and Video.)

San Diego Union.
    1986.   "Beyond the pale." Editorial. March 14.

Schwietz, Jackie.
    1987.   *   Speech at workshop on "School-Based Clinics: Ways to Counter—
               State and Local." National Right to Life annual convention,
               June 18, in New Orleans, Louisiana. (Audio cassette recording
               of conference tape number 8 purchased from Cincinnati Right
               to Life.)

Scientists' Institute for Public Information.
    1986.   *   *Preventing Adolescent Pregnancy: A Symposium for Journal-
               ists.* New York. (May 14, 1986).

Seligmann, Jean, et al.
1987.   "A Challenge to School Clinics." *Newsweek*, August 10.

Senderwitz, Judith.
1987.   "Viewpoint: Debating School Clinics." *Miami Herald*, August 2.

Shaheen, Paul.
1986.   Speech at plenary session on "SBCs: Capturing Public Funds."
             National School-Based Clinic conference, October 6, in Denver,
             Colorado. (Audio tape recording by Richard D. Glasow—not
             for sale.)

1987.   *   Speech at workshop on "Comprehensive Adolescent Health
             Services: Advocacy Strategies." National conference of the
             Children's Defense Fund, March 13, in Washington, D.C..
             (Audio cassette recording of conference tape number 22 pur-
             chased from Visual Aids Electronics.)

Shipp, E.R.
1985.   "Debate Over Sex and a School Clinic." *New York Times*.
             September 22.

Silva, Mark.
1987.   "Governor blocks money for health clinic." *Miami Herald*, July
             22.

Spitz, Irving M. and Wayne Bardin.
1985.   "Antiprogestins: Prospects for a Once-a-Month Pill." *Family
             Planning Perspectives* 17 (6):260-262 (November/December).

St. Martin, John.
1986.   "Pro-Abortionists Look To Counter Pro-Life Trend Among
             Youth." *National Right to Life News*, September 25.

Steele, Marilyn.
1986.   "Teen pregnancy: a foundation perspective." *Planned Parent-
             hood Review* 6 (2):11-12 (Spring).

Stephen, Beverly.
1986.   "Teens who wait: Effort underway to curb pregnancies." *[New
             York] Daily News*, April 17.

Sullivan, Ellen, Christopher Tietze, and Joy G. Dryfoos.
   1977.   "Legal Abortion in the United States, 1975-1976." *Family
             Planning Perspectives* 9 (3):116-117, 121, 124-129 (May/June).

Teltsch, Kathleen.
   1986.   "Grants Increase For Work in Population Area." *New York
             Times*, May 19.

Thomas, John B.
   1987.   "Dissenters want names off teen clinic report." *Alexandria
             [Virginia] Gazette Packet*, July 24-28.

Times-West Virginian.
   1986.   December 3.

U.S. Congress. House.
   1985.   Select Committee on Children, Youth and Families. *Teen Preg-
             nancy: What is Being Done? A state-by-state look.* 99th Cong.,
             1st sess.. Committee print. December.

   1987a.   *A bill To amend the Public Health Service Act to establish
             school-based adolescent health services demonstration projects.*
             H.R. 1609. 100th Cong., 1st sess. March 12. Sections 2307(a)(3)
             and 2310.

   1987b.   *A bill To Authorize the Secretary of Education to make grants
             to local educational agencies for dropout prevention and reentry
             demonstration projects.* H.R. 738, 100th Cong., 1st sess., Janu-
             ary 26.

   1987c.   Committee on Energy and Commerce. Subcommittee on Health
             and the Environment. *Hearing on School-Based Health Clinic
             Programs.* 100th Cong., 1st sess., June 5.

U.S. Congress. Senate.
   1981.   Committee on Labor and Human Resources. *Oversight of Fam-
             ily Planning Programs, 1981: Hearing.* 97th Cong., 1st sess.,
             March 31.

   1982a.   Committee on Judiciary, Subcommittee on Separation of Pow-
             ers. *Hearings on the Human Life Bill, S. 158,* Appendix. 97th
             Cong., 1st Sess., Serial No. J-97-16.

1982b.   Committee on the Judiciary. *Human Life Federalism Amend-ment: Report on S.J. 110.* 97th Cong., 2d sess., S. Rpt. 97-465. June 8.

1983.   Committee on the Judiciary. Subcommittee on the Constitu-tion. *Hearings on Constitutional Amendments Relating To Abortion.* 97th Cong., lst sess.. Serial No. J-97-62. Vol. 2.

1987.   *A bill To Authorize the Secretary of Education to make grants to local educational agencies for dropout prevention and reentry demonstration projects.* S. 320. 100th Cong., 1st sess., January 16.

U.S. Department of Health and Human Services.
1981.   *Program Guidelines for Project Grants For Family Planning Services.* Health Services Administration, Bureau of Commun-ity Health Services, Office of Family Planning. Second edition.

1987.   "Statutory Prohibition on Use of Appropriated Funds in Pro-grams Where Abortion Is a Method of Family Planning; Stand-ard of Compliance for Family Planning Services Projects." Pro-posed Rules. *Federal Register,* volume 52, number 169 (Sep-tember 1), pages 33210 through 33215.

U. S. GAO.
1986.   Government Accounting Office. Letter from Richard L. Fogel, Asst. Comptroller General, to U.S. Senator Jesse Helms, Serial HR6-147, December 22.

U. S. National Center for Health Statistics. Department of Health and Human Services.
1985   "Advance Report of Final Natality Statistics, 1983." *Monthly Vital Statistics Report* 34 (6) Supplement.

Viadero, Debra.
1986.   "Clinics' Birth-Control Efforts Aim to Control Growth in Black Population, Some Charge." *Education Week.* 7 (10):1,12,13 (November 12).

Wagner, Kathleen.
1986.   "Case Study: Teen Clinic, Washington, D.C.." *Family Protec-tion Report* (January).

Wallis, Claudia.
1985.   "Children Having Children." *TIME*, December 9.

Wardle, Lynn and Mary Anne Q. Wood.
1982.   *A Lawyer Looks At Abortion*. Provo, Utah: Brigham Young
           University Press.

Wattleton, Faye.
1981.   "Statement." In U.S. Congress. Senate. 1981.

1982.   Speech presented at "President's Panel" session of the annual
           meeting of the Association of Planned Parenthood Profession-
           als, November 19, in Baltimore, Maryland. (Audio cassette
           recording of conference tape number 3 purchased from Visual
           Aids Electronics.)

1986.   "Are high-school health clinics appropriate for teenagers? Yes."
           [Dover] Delaware State News, May 4. Scripps-Howard News
           Service. Also carried in *[Ontario, CA] Report*, May 29, as "U.S.
           Needs Health Clinics in Schools."

Weed, Stan E.
1986.   "Curbing Births, Not Pregnancies." *Wall Street Journal*, Octo-
           ber 14.

Willke, John C.
1987.   Personal communication.

Wunsch, Bobbie and Barbara Aved.
1987.   "Trends in Health Care Financing: Opportunities for Family
           Planning Agencies." *Family Planning Perspectives* 19 (2):71-74
           (March/April).

Yorkey, Mike.
1986.   "SBCs On the Move." *Focus on the Family with Dr. James
           Dobson* 10 (10):2-5 (October).

Zabin, Laurie.
1986a.   "An Evaluation of Inner-City Schools Linked with a Pregnancy
           Prevention Program." Speech at plenary session on "Research
           Update." National School-Based Clinic conference, October 7,
           in Denver, Colorado. (Audio tape recording by Richard D.
           Glasow—not for sale.)

1986b.   "The School-Based Approach to Teen Pregnancy Prevention."
           Planned Parenthood Review 6 (2):8-9 (Spring).

Zabin, Laurie S. et al.
    1984.   "A School-, Hospital- and University-Based Adolescent Preg-
              nancy Prevention Program." *Journal of Reproductive Health* 29
              (6):421-426.

    1986.   "Evaluation of a Pregnancy Prevention Program for Urban
              Teenagers." *Family Planning Perspectives* 18 (3):119-126 (May/
              June).

Zanga, Joseph, M.D.
    1986.   * Speech presented at workshop on "School-Based Clinics, Part
             I." Annual meeting of the American Public Health Assn.,
             October 6, in Las Vegas, Nevada. (Audio cassette recording of
             conference tape number 1067 purchased from Audio Recording
             Services.)

Zlatos, Bill.
    1986.   "Split over sex data at school clinics runs deep." *Pittsburgh
              Press*, September 14.

Sources for Hard-to-Find Publications and Audio Tapes

American Audio Association
Box 511
Floral Park, NY 11002
Phone: (212) 740-0186

Archdiocese of Boston
Family Life Office
2121 Commonwealth Avenue
Brighton, MA 02135
Phone: (619) 783-2451

Audio Recording Services,
4406 W. Charleston Blvd.
Las Vegas, NV89102
Phone: (702) 870-0947

Castle Sound and Video, Inc.
2702 Maretello Drive
Silver Spring, MD20904

Center for Population Options
1012 14th Street, N.W. Suite 1200
Washington, D.C. 20005

Cincinnati Right to Life
P.O. Box 24073
Cincinnati, OH 45224
Phone: (513) 522-0820

Family Research Council
515 Second St., N.E.
Washington, D.C. 20002
Phone: (202) 546-5400

Healthstart, Inc.
640 Jackson Street
St. Paul, MN55101
Phone: (619) 221-3422

National Academy Press
2100 Pennsylvania Ave, N.W.
Room 700
Washington, D.C. 20418

Scientists' Institute for Public
    Information
355 Lexington Avenue
New York, NY 10017
Phone: (212) 661-9110 or
    (800) 223-1730

Visual Aids Electronics
2831 15th St., N.W.
Washington, D.C. 20009

To order more copies of . . .

SCHOOL-BASED CLINICS, THE ABORTION CONNECTION

. . . use this order form

✂

Quantity	Price
1	$2.95 ea.
2-5	2.65 ea.
6-9	2.50 ea.
10+	2.35 ea.

Please send me _____ copies of
**SCHOOL-BASED CLINICS,
THE ABORTION CONNECTION**

Total $ _____

Terms and Conditions

1. Payment by check, money order or bank card (MasterCard or Visa) must accompany orders. Bank card orders—minimum of $20.00. Prices include postage and handling.

2. Make checks payable to NRL Educational Trust Fund.

3. Mail to NRL Educational Trust Fund, 419 7th St. N.W., Suite 500, Washington, D.C. 20004.

4. Telephone orders—payment by bank card only. Call (202) 626-8809

5. Schools, libraries, churches, book stores, and NRL's associated state organization's offices may request billing.

6. Shipments are made by United Parcel Service (UPS). **Please give street address.** Allow three (3) weeks for delivery.

DATE REQUIRED: _____

BILL TO: _____
_____
_____

Street Address for UPS Delivery

SHIP TO: _____
_____
_____

☎ **Rush Order? Pay By Credit Card. Phone Us! (202) 626-8809**

☐ Enclosed is my check or money order for Total Payment Due
☐ Charge my Total Payment due to my credit card.
☐ MasterCard   ☐ Visa

Card No. _____

Expiration Date _____

Printed Name of Card Holder _____

Address of Card Holder _____

To order more copies of . . .

SCHOOL-BASED CLINICS, THE ABORTION CONNECTION

. . . use this order form

✂

Quantity	Price
1	$2.95 ea.
2-5	2.65 ea.
6-9	2.50 ea.
10+	2.35 ea.

Please send me _____ copies of

SCHOOL-BASED CLINICS, THE ABORTION CONNECTION

Total $ _____

Terms and Conditions

1. Payment by check, money order or bank card (MasterCard or Visa) must accompany orders. Bank card orders—minimum of $20.00. Prices include postage and handling.

2. Make checks payable to NRL Educational Trust Fund.

3. Mail to NRL Educational Trust Fund, 419 7th St. N.W., Suite 500, Washington, D.C. 20004.

4. Telephone orders—payment by bank card only. Call (202) 626-8809.

5. Schools, libraries, churches, book stores, and NRL's associated state organization's offices may request billing.

6. Shipments are made by United Parcel Service (UPS). Please give street address. Allow three (3) weeks for delivery.

DATE REQUIRED: _____

BILL TO: _____

_____

_____

Street Address for UPS Delivery

SHIP TO: _____

_____

_____

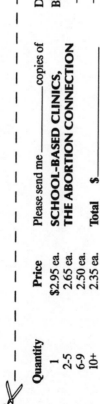 **Rush Order? Pay By Credit Card. Phone Us!** (202) 626-8809

☐ Enclosed is my check or money order for Total Payment Due
☐ Charge my Total Payment due to my credit card.
☐ MasterCard   ☐ Visa

Card No. _____

Expiration Date _____

Printed Name of Card Holder _____

Address of Card Holder _____

To order more copies of . . .

SCHOOL–BASED CLINICS, THE ABORTION CONNECTION

. . . use this order form

Quantity	Price
1	$2.95 ea.
2-5	2.65 ea.
6-9	2.50 ea.
10+	2.35 ea.

Please send me _____ copies of

SCHOOL-BASED CLINICS,
THE ABORTION CONNECTION

Total $ _____

Terms and Conditions

1. Payment by check, money order or bank card (MasterCard or Visa) must accompany orders. Bank card orders—minimum of $20.00. Prices include postage and handling.

2. Make checks payable to NRL Educational Trust Fund.

3. Mail to NRL Educational Trust Fund, 419 7th St. N.W., Suite 500, Washington, D.C. 20004.

4. Telephone orders—payment by bank card only. Call (202) 626-8809

5. Schools, libraries, churches, book stores, and NRL's associated state organization's offices may request billing.

6. Shipments are made by United Parcel Service (UPS). Please give street address. Allow three (3) weeks for delivery.

DATE REQUIRED: _____

BILL TO: _____

Street Address for UPS Delivery

SHIP TO: _____

☎ **Rush Order? Pay By Credit Card. Phone Us! (202) 626-8809**

☐ Enclosed is my check or money order for Total Payment Due
☐ Charge my Total Payment due to my credit card.
☐ MasterCard   ☐ Visa

Card No. _____

Expiration Date _____

Printed Name of Card Holder _____

Address of Card Holder _____